A book for
Family Reading

A SAD LITTLE DOG!

A book for
Family Reading

A
Sᴀᴅ
Lɪᴛᴛʟᴇ Dᴏɢ!

Fifty-two stories that teach biblical truths

Jim Cromarty

 EVANGELICAL PRESS

EVANGELICAL PRESS
Faverdale North Industrial Estate, Darlington, DL3 0PH, England

Evangelical Press USA
P. O. Box 84, Auburn, MA 01501, USA

e-mail: sales@evangelical-press.org

web: http://www.evangelicalpress.org

First published 2000

British Library Cataloguing in Publication Data available

ISBN 0 85234 463 5

Printed and bound in Great Britain by Creative Print & Design Wales, Ebbw Vale

To the late Bill Clark:
one meeting with him changed my life.

Contents

Preface

This volume marks the seventh in the series of books for family reading (if we include *A Book for Family Worship*). It is our prayer that God will bless what has been written to the hearts of all who have read the books, and our hope that the series might be instrumental in establishing daily devotions in families that were strangers to such a practice.

In 1993 the idea for such a series was planted in my mind by the late Bill Clark, who was visiting Australia. I was most unwell and a Baptist pastor — a friend for many years — called at our home. He was escorting Bill up the coast of New South Wales and the meeting proved to be providential. Because of my health, my ministry with my congregation had come to an end and to me the future looked bleak. However, God is sovereign and now, more than ever, I know the truth of those precious words in Romans 8:28: 'And we know that all things work together for good to those who love God, to those who are the called according to his purpose.'

Over a 'cup of tea' Bill enquired what I was doing. Soon we were in my study, where he read one of my stories and suggested I forward a selection of them to Evangelical Press for assessment, with the result that the first of the Family Reading books, *How to cook a crow*, was published.

My prayer was that God would give me the ability to write sufficient stories in order that families might have a year's supply of material for family devotions. With this, the seventh volume, that prayer has now been answered! The books do not follow a pattern requiring their use in any particular order.

My wife Val has been my proof-reader; my brother John and his wife Elizabeth have read the manuscripts and made suggestions for improvement. Thanks go to these and others for their assistance and motivation.

To all who read my books, I would urge you to read the Scriptures faithfully, spend time in prayer, read good Christian publications and mix with God's people at every opportunity.

We have a wonderful God, who freely gave his Son, the Lord Jesus Christ, as a sacrificial offering for the sins of his people. Let us show the world that we love our God and glorify our Saviour in all that we say and do.

May God bless you all, and may parents have the joy of seeing their children come to saving faith in Christ through the gracious work of the Holy Spirit in their hearts.

I should like to thank all those people who took the time to write to me. We now have a lovely collection of postcards from many parts of the world. Three of the books have now been translated into Russian and for this I praise God.

Finally, I thank my God for his grace in making possible this form of ministry. May God be pleased to use these books to edify his people and win sinners into the kingdom of his one and only beloved Son, the Lord Jesus Christ, to whom be all the glory.

Jim Cromarty

Fishing

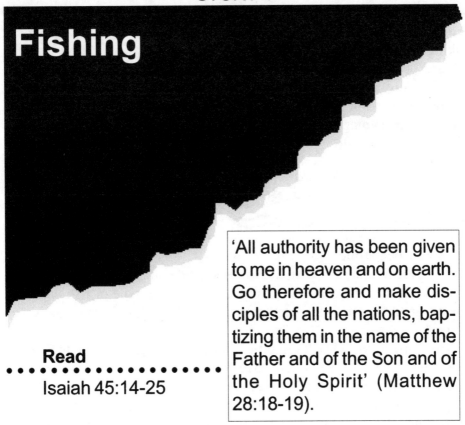

Read
• • • • • • • • • • • • • • • • •
Isaiah 45:14-25

'All authority has been given to me in heaven and on earth. Go therefore and make disciples of all the nations, baptizing them in the name of the Father and of the Son and of the Holy Spirit' (Matthew 28:18-19).

Fishing is an enjoyable sport. Most of the time it means quietness and plenty of time to think. Try and imagine a peaceful day beside the river, sitting in the shade under a tree, the wind blowing gently and the fish biting. At the end of the day there is usually some fish to take home. Yes, fishing can be a peaceful sport.

Once I tried trout fishing which meant wading out in the cold water. Fly fishing is difficult and I discovered that a day standing in the cool water is not the best way to enjoy a holiday. However the fish were biting and it made the time worthwhile.

Then there were those occasions when we went out to sea, launching our boat on the beach and shooting out to the open sea through the breaking waves risking life and limb. On one occasion we capsized out at sea and that proved to be a frightening morning. But usually the result was rewarding as we returned home with a good catch of big fish.

Before setting out on our fishing expeditions we spent time studying the weather forecast, the winds and tides and making sure we had a variety of the best baits. The bait that caught one type of fish was not always good for another species. We always took our fishing trips very seriously.

The Lord Jesus, when calling Peter and his brother Andrew to follow him said, 'Follow me, and I will make you fishers of men' (Matthew 4:19). They, with the other disciples, were men who would 'catch' sinners with the gospel of salvation. Today all Christians should be fishermen for Christ. Presenting the gospel to lost sinners is a serious business. It means that the Word of God must be studied, so that gospel truths may be known and understood. And just as fishermen use different baits for different varieties

of fish, so also it is necessary to present Christ to people in different ways. What appeals to some people is not attractive to others. Some people are attracted to Christ when they hear of God's great love, while others run to Christ when they hear they are doomed because of their sins.

Just as fishermen must get out and work at catching fish, so also Christians must become involved in the work of confessing Christ to the world. Some people are called to become missionaries, others pastors of settled congregations, some to be Sunday school teachers, and most to witness to Christ where they work and live. Fishermen do not sit at home and expect the fish to crawl out of the water and find their way to the dinner table. The same applies to the church. Sinners don't want Christ and salvation and this means that Christians must go to them. Some godly people will pray that God will bless the word spoken by those who take the good news to sinners. Others will give finance to support Christian work. There are many tasks to be carried out supporting those who go into Satan's territory.

You can read of men and women who risked everything in order to preach Christ. The story of John Paton and his wife is well worth reading. They took the gospel to the cannibals of the New Hebrides. John's new wife Mary and son Peter died, and he was driven from the island by men who wanted to have him killed. However, he so loved the people of that region that he returned again preaching the gospel of Christ.

Many missionaries lived like the people to whom they took the gospel. Hudson Taylor dressed like the Chinese and spoke their language. They put into practice what Paul had done. He wrote: 'I have become all things to all men, that I might by all means save some' (1 Corinthians 9:22). They became part of the community to whom they preached the gospel. They dressed like the people, worked with the people, helped those in need and so won the affection of sinners. Life for those missionaries was very difficult, but they loved the Lord Jesus more than they loved their own lives. They knew that the people needed to hear the good news concerning salvation through faith in God's Son, the Lord Jesus Christ. The promise of God encouraged them to risk everything for their Saviour: 'For as the rain comes down, and the snow from heaven, and do not return there, but water the earth, and make it bring forth and bud, that it may give seed to the sower and bread to the eater, so shall my word be that goes forth from my mouth; it shall not return to me void, but it shall accomplish what I please, and it shall prosper in the thing for which I sent it' (Isaiah 55:10-11).

Some Christians planted the word, others came along and reinforced what had been said, while others saw men and women converted when they spoke of Christ. What some people believed to be total foolishness, to others it was 'the power of God' to salvation (1 Corinthians 1:18). Every Christian has a part to play, no matter how small, in spreading the good news concerning the Lord Jesus. They are to be like fishermen who take their sport seriously.

Remember today's text. You will witness to the Saviour you love, in his strength. He has all power in heaven and on the earth. This should give you confidence in every aspect of your Christian life. Pray that God will revive his work and give his people a harvest of souls to praise and glorify him.

Those who sow in tears
Shall reap in joy.
He who continually goes forth weeping,
Bearing seed for sowing,
Shall doubtless come again with rejoicing,
Bringing his sheaves with him

(Psalm 126:5-6).

To think about

1. How can you become involved in witnessing to Christ's salvation?
2. How does your pastor witness to the saving work of Christ?
3. How could the following people witness for Christ?
   a. A Christian in hospital; b. A mother with three little children; c. A Christian schoolteacher; d. A boy playing football; e. A Christian politician.

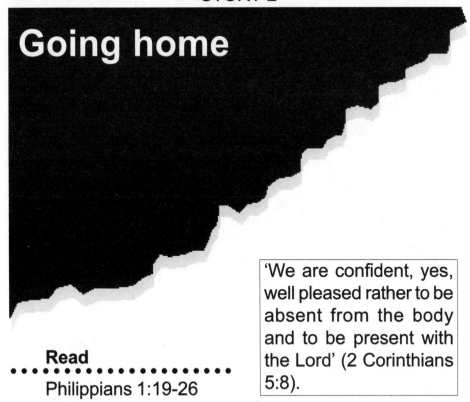

Going home

'We are confident, yes, well pleased rather to be absent from the body and to be present with the Lord' (2 Corinthians 5:8).

Read
● ● ● ● ● ● ● ● ● ● ● ● ● ● ● ● ● ●
Philippians 1:19-26

People don't like talking about dying, yet this event is a certainty for each one of us, unless the Lord returns before the day of our death. Children die as well as elderly people, so all should be prepared for the day when we lie down for the final time.

Recently I conducted the funeral of a man who was not a Christian. What could I say? He had been a fine, moral citizen who cared for his family and was always ready to help people in need. However, he was a stranger to Christ and was doomed to everlasting punishment. His death was so different to a dear Christian friend, who passed into glory with a true peace in his heart because he was a friend of the Lord Jesus Christ. As death is going home to be with the Lord, Christians should never fear it.

Many years ago we lived in a schoolhouse. It was a comfortable home, but as it needed repairs we looked forward to the day when we would have our own place. The day came when we purchased our plot of land and the plans for our new home were drawn up. We decided what we needed for our family and made our plans just as we had discussed for years.

Each member of the family was very excited about the prospects of moving to a new area and at long last living in a home we could call our own. We talked about the carpet we would put on the floor, the children discussed what wallpaper they wanted in their rooms, Val picked out the kitchen she

15

would like built and I planned what I would like in my study.

The day finally arrived for us to move and everyone was so excited. The lawns had been mown, the gardens were taking shape and the furniture had been packed by the removal men. We said farewell to our friends, saying that we'd see them all again one day, and drove to our new residence. Our joy was tinged with the sadness of leaving our old home and friends behind, but we were looking forward to meeting the surrounding neighbours and making a new set of friends.

Our new home was very comfortable. I had my study with plenty of shelves for my books, Val had the kitchen she'd always wanted and the girls were so pleased with their new rooms.

Since those days I've always thought of death as a day of leaving my earthly home and being taken to a new residence, perfectly designed and built, in heaven. The day of our passing should hold no fears for all who have trusted their salvation to the Lord Jesus Christ.

In the story of the rich man and Lazarus (Luke 16:19-31) we read that when Lazarus died, God's angels escorted him to heaven. Lazarus left a world where he was a nobody, starving in the street outside the home of a rich man. He was taken to 'Abraham's bosom', to heaven! I'm sure that Lazarus had no fear of going to be with God and living in the land of perfection where there would be no hunger or sadness.

It was God who sent his angels to escort Lazarus into his presence. This truth should comfort all Christians when they think about death and when they face their own passing. The psalmist wrote, 'Precious in the sight of the Lord is the death of his saints' (Psalm 116:15).

The apostle Paul had no fear of death for he knew it meant going home to be with Christ. In today's reading we find his confident, longing words, 'For to me, to live is Christ, and to die is gain.' Paul had a desire to be with Christ, which he knew would be far better than anything the world had to offer him. He would have known the promise of Christ to the disciples, 'Let not your heart be troubled; you believe in God, believe also in me. In my Father's house are many mansions … I go to prepare a place for you' (John 14:1-3).

For Christians, death, although our enemy, is an event that is full of hope, because it has been defeated by the risen Lord Jesus. Our faith looks beyond this world and all of its troubles, to our Saviour sitting upon the throne of God. Dying, as far as the Christian is concerned, is going home to be with Christ and that means rest from the difficulties we daily face on earth. Christians are able to say, with the apostle Paul, 'We are confident, yes, well pleased rather to be absent from the body and to be present with the Lord' (2 Corinthians 5:8).

Christians! Anticipate the joy of being with Christ in the heavenly kingdom he has prepared for his people. Meditate upon the precious words that follow.

Yea, though I walk through the valley of the shadow of death,
I will fear no evil;
For you are with me;
Your rod and your staff, they comfort me

(Psalm 23:4).

To think about

1. Why will Christians be happy in heaven?
2. Why was the apostle Paul unafraid of dying?
3. Why is heaven 'home' to God's people?
4. What did Jesus mean when he said to his disciples: 'In my Father's house are many mansions; if it were not so, I would have told you. I go to prepare a place for you' (John 14:2).
5. The Bible describes Christians as 'pilgrims' on this earth. Why? (See Hebrews 11:13 and 1 Peter 2:11.)

A majestic return

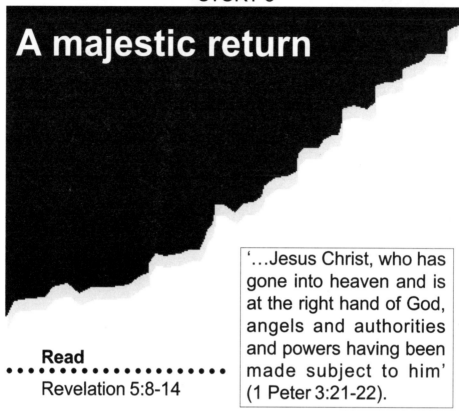

Read
• • • • • • • • • • • • • • • • • • •
Revelation 5:8-14

'...Jesus Christ, who has gone into heaven and is at the right hand of God, angels and authorities and powers having been made subject to him' (1 Peter 3:21-22).

'Winners are grinners' is an expression commonly heard today. There is a lot of rejoicing by winning teams but not much cheering done by the losers.

Last year the Australian football team from my childhood district won the Sydney competition for the first time. They were known as 'the Knights' and their flag has the picture of a mounted knight going out to fight. It was a hard game and both sides suffered injuries. While all the local people hoped

they would win, some had doubts as the opposing team was in excellent form. After eighty minutes of strenuous play the Knights and their supporters were able to cheer and stamp their feet. After the game, which was played in Sydney, the Knights made a triumphal return to their Newcastle clubhouse, with cheering faithful supporters lining the highway and streets for many miles.

As the players stepped out of the bus it was easy to see the injuries many of the players had sustained. There were bruises, black eyes, scratches and deep cuts; some were limping while several had their wounds covered by band aids and bandages. They carried the marks of the battle, but they were smiling and waving to their supporters because they were winners! They had returned to their club as victors! The trophy was held high and the huge clubhouse was filled with cheering and clapping.

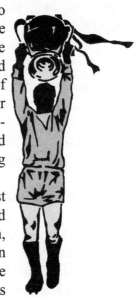

At the time I began to think of the Lord Jesus Christ returning to heaven as the conquering hero. He had fought a battle with 'the Prince of this world', Satan, and was victorious. The Lord Jesus had defeated Satan by dying as the sin bearer. He was punished in the place of his people, died and was buried. He carried to his tomb the marks of the battle — the nail prints in his hands and feet, a scar on his side where he was wounded by a soldier's spear, the deep cuts from the crown of thorns and the marks where the whip had cut into his back.

When Christ came forth from the tomb he still carried the marks of his battle with the Prince of Darkness. Thomas wouldn't believe that the disciples had seen the risen Lord. However, a week later, when the Lord Jesus appeared, he spoke to Thomas, 'Reach your finger here, and look at my hands; and reach your hand here, and put it into my side. Do not be unbelieving, but believing' (John 20:27). The risen Christ still carried the scars of his warfare!

In the last chapter I wrote about death and our going home to be with our Saviour. Now we are looking at the Redeemer's return to his heavenly home. Carrying the marks of the conflict he ascended to heaven where he took his place on God's throne. This was a glorious homecoming for the Lord of glory. He truly is 'King of kings and Lord of lords' (Revelation 19:16). The inhabitants of heaven sang the praises of the risen Lord: 'Worthy is the Lamb who was slain to receive power and riches and wisdom, and strength and honour and glory and blessing! … Blessing and honour and glory and power be to him who sits on the throne, and to the Lamb, forever and ever' (Revelation 5:12-13).

Our Saviour was given his seat on the right side of the throne, the place of honour and authority (Hebrews 1:3). The risen Saviour was not only seen as the Lamb of God who died as the sacrificial offering on the cross, but also as 'the Lion of the tribe of Judah' (Revelation 5:5). The heavenly hosts — angels and the saints — praised the returning Lord of glory. This was a wonderful occasion in the history of eternity!

When the glorified Lord sat down upon his throne of glory the great archangel Michael and his angelic army threw Satan out of heaven. No longer could the devil appear before the throne of God to accuse the saints. Our Redeemer had once and for all triumphed over Satan, and the saints had every right to be in heaven for Christ had won their salvation.

Now in heaven, Messiah, the only Mediator between God and man, presents our prayers to his Father and distributes blessings to sinners. Let all who confess Christ as their Lord and Saviour praise him in both speech and life. We have a wonderful Saviour!

> Lift up your heads, O you gates!
> And be lifted up, you everlasting doors!
> And the King of glory shall come in…
> Who is this King of glory?
> The Lord of hosts,
> He is the King of glory

(Psalm 24:7,10).

To think about

1. The precious words in the psalm quoted above speak of what event in David's life? Read 2 Samuel 6:12-19.
2. Talk about an event where you received praise for success. How did it feel?
3. If you are a Christian, what will be the reason for your entrance into heaven?
4. What work is Christ now carrying out in heaven?

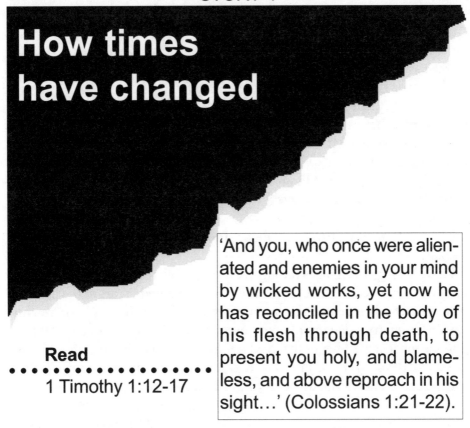

How times have changed

Read
• • • • • • • • • • • • • • • •
1 Timothy 1:12-17

'And you, who once were alienated and enemies in your mind by wicked works, yet now he has reconciled in the body of his flesh through death, to present you holy, and blameless, and above reproach in his sight...' (Colossians 1:21-22).

There is no doubt times have changed! Things are not what they used to be and from today's reading you will notice that great changes took place in the life of a Pharisee named Saul. He became the apostle Paul, a faithful servant of the Lord Jesus Christ. He was able to say that he received mercy from the one he once hated and whose followers he persecuted.

Saul had a great future as a leader of the Pharisees, but all was different when the Lord interrupted his journey to Damascus. He had once boasted that he was a Jew of the tribe of Benjamin, circumcised according to the law of God and a member of the Pharisees — that group of men who believed they were truly faithful to the law of God (Philippians 3:4-6). Towards the end of his life he wrote that he had received mercy from God, the forgiveness of sins and eternal life. How life had changed for the apostle Paul!

I'm sure that each one of us can look back and see how our life has become different. Elderly people often speak about the great changes they have experienced during their lives. I can well remember travelling about in a horse and sulky driven by my grandfather who never owned or drove a car.

In my childhood I'd never heard of a television, but I listened to the wireless (radio) each day. We milked the cows by hand for many years and I can remember Dad and Grandfather ploughing the land using a horse and plough. I can even remember them 'broadcasting' the seed as they walked back and forth across the ploughed ground. Today these jobs are done by machinery.

Try and imagine Mr Cruden preparing his *Bible Concordance*. He must have had thousands of pages on which he wrote his many words. This task took him many years of painstaking labour. Today a computer can do the job in minutes!

I have seen great changes during my lifetime, but recently something was said that convinced me that times really have changed. Years ago when my children met other people the comment was often made, 'Oh, you're Jim and Val Cromarty's daughter.' I was reasonably well known because I was a schoolteacher, a member of the local town council and active in the church.

Several days ago I was introduced to some locals and after some discussion the comment was made, 'Oh, you're Heather Wilson's father.' Heather

is well known in the community and I'm no longer known by some people, except as Heather's father. Suddenly I became aware of the fact that times have changed. I am getting old and a new generation occupies the stage of history.

I look at myself and see the changes that have taken place. My hair has thinned, my waistline has become bigger, I'm not as healthy as I used to be and I need my spectacles to read. If you have a look at a photograph taken of yourself some years ago you will notice the many differences.

The greatest change in my life is that whereas once I lived for myself I am now a Christian and delight in the things of the Lord Jesus. There was a time when I was 'dead in trespasses and sins', but now I am alive in Christ

(Ephesians 2:1). This is true of millions of other people — once strangers to Christ, but now his friends through his sacrifice upon the cross. Instead of being responsible citizens of Satan's kingdom they are now sons and daughters of the living God and members of his kingdom. Instead of enjoying a sinful life they have turned their back on unrighteousness and practise holiness.

Yes, times have changed. However, the real question you must face is this: 'Am I different?' Has God touched your heart? On Judgement Day will you face Christ as a friend or as one who will condemn you because of your sins?

May you be able to look back on your life and say concerning your relationship with Christ, 'I am a new person! Whereas once I was lost, I am now found. I'm saved by the redeeming work of Christ.'

The words of the hymn 'Amazing Grace' should thrill your soul:

Amazing grace! How sweet the sound,
That saved a wretch like me!
I once was lost, but now am found,
Was blind, but now I see.

John Newton (1725-1807)

But as for me, I trust in you, O LORD;
I say, 'You are my God.'
My times are in your hand;
Deliver me from the hand of my enemies,
And from those who persecute me

(Psalm 31:14-15).

To think about

1. Discuss some of the obvious ways you (or some family member) have changed over the years.
2. In what way has God changed you?
3. What parable told by Christ speaks of seed being sown? Read Matthew 13:3-9, 18-23. Who were the people who saw permanent changes in their lives?

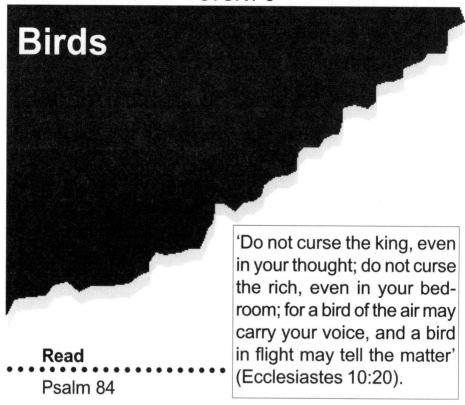

Birds

> 'Do not curse the king, even in your thought; do not curse the rich, even in your bedroom; for a bird of the air may carry your voice, and a bird in flight may tell the matter' (Ecclesiastes 10:20).

Read
••••••••••••••••••••
Psalm 84

Yesterday I spoke to a friend I had not met for some time. We had so much to tell each other that we sat down and talked for a long time as we drank several cups of coffee. Then he told me something about myself that I was sure no one knew. I asked him, 'How did you discover that?' His reply was

a common expression, 'A little bird told me!'

Today's text is the place from which that expression came. Here we are reminded that even our closest secrets are not true secrets at all. We tell one person our secret and what we say is overheard. Soon others are told what was a private matter. Even if I keep the matter to myself, God knows. When our secret words become known and we don't know how this happened we can say, 'A little bird told them!' In our text we are told that a little bird who overheard a cruel word revealed what was said in private.

We learn a lot about birds as we study God's Word. Our reading speaks of the little sparrow who made a nest in the tabernacle where there was security for her family. We read about the eagle and discover that it hovers over the nest to protect its young. When the eaglet is being taught to fly the adult bird carries it into the sky on its strong wings (Deuteronomy 32:11). This is a beautiful picture of God who protects and cares for his people because he loves each one of them. It is in his strength that we fight the battles of faith. As you go about your activities you will see many birds. Look closely at their habits and you may make interesting discoveries.

When John and I were recently out fishing we saw many sea birds resting near the ocean wall on which we were standing. The pelican, 'whose beak

can hold more than their belly can', seemed to be taking it easy, just looking about them. Maybe they were dreaming about a feed of fish. When the rain began to fall, John noticed that all the pelicans turned to face the falling rain. They opened their huge beaks and allowed the drops of rain to fall into their open mouths. The pelican lives in a region where there is a lot of salt water and possibly fresh water is in short supply. When we saw the birds drinking the fresh rain John quoted the words of Psalm 81:10: 'I am the LORD your God, who brought you out of the land of Egypt; open your mouth wide, and I will fill it.'

We have a generous God who provides for the needs of his creation. Although sinful men and women have damaged the creation, God still gives.

His greatest gift was his Son, the Lord Jesus Christ, who said of his heavenly Father, 'For God so loved the world that he gave his only begotten Son, that whoever believes in him should not perish but have everlasting life' (John 3:16).

Another bird that should remind people of the debts they owe God is the black and white magpie. These birds love worms and grubs and can be seen walking about and looking for food on the grass, especially where it has been mown.

There are times when they get into the garden and scratch about in the earth looking for worms. Often, when they find one they gobble it down and then raise their head to heaven and warble. It seems as if they gaze towards God and offer thanks to their Creator for providing their food.

We can learn from the magpie and offer thanks to God for all that he has given us — our food, homes, loved ones, clothing, occupations, abilities and most of all for providing us with a Saviour.

There are also animals that unknowingly help birds find their food. Have you seen the egret, that white bird with long legs that often is seen either standing on the back of a cow or bull or walking about near the animal's head as it grazes? The egret is waiting for the animal to disturb insects that live in the grass. When this happens they quickly snap up their food. This should remind us that we are to be kind to one another, helping whenever we can. We can learn so much from the birds and animals about us.

> For every beast of the forest is mine,
> And the cattle on a thousand hills.
> I know all the birds of the mountains,
> And the wild beasts of the field are mine
>
> (Psalm 50:10-11).

To think about

1. Make a list of five birds mentioned in the Bible.
2. Our reading indicated that the sparrow found security in the tabernacle. In what way do we find security in the church? What is the biblical meaning of the 'church'?
3. What bird is common to Noah and the baptism of Jesus? Read Genesis 8:8 and John 1:32, but not before you have thought about the question.

Where's my house?

Read
• • • • • • • • • • • • • • • • • •
Lamentations 2:5-8
and Luke 21:20-24

'He has done violence to his tabernacle, as if it were a garden; he has destroyed his place of assembly; the Lord has caused the appointed feasts and Sabbaths to be forgotten in Zion. In his burning indignation he has spurned the king and the priest' (Lamentations 2:6).

There are many buildings in Wingham that I consider to be important — some are of historical value and worthy of care. I was once a member of the local council and we met in the town hall for our monthly meetings. This old building is an important structure which has a tower from which is flown the

Australian flag. Four clocks face the four corners of the globe. Sadly the clocks do not tell the same time, but the town hall can be seen from most parts of town. Each year the council spends money to ensure the town hall is kept in good order. The police station, the school and several old buildings are all considered important by the local community.

However, there are two buildings that I admire. First is the

building where our church members gather to worship God. We all know that the building is just pieces of timber and that the church is really the members of the congregation who are Christians, but we make sure our building is kept in good repair as it is most important in the life of the congregation.

The other building that I enjoy is our home. It is not just a house, but Val and I have made it into a home. It contains the possessions that God has seen fit to give to us, but most important, it is the building in which we live. It is a happy home  and when our daughters visit us they find many items that remind them of happy times they had when growing up. I'd hate to see our residence destroyed!

Some time ago I read in the paper of a very upset couple who had just arrived home to find their house destroyed. The police were present and there was a lot of talk going on between them and a man who stood beside a bulldozer. The shocked couple soon found out that the house several blocks  away was to be pulled down to make way for a new, two-storey house. The driver of the bulldozer had won the contract to de-molish the house that was No. 32 Jackson Street, but someone had given him a contract which read No. 22 Jackson Street. He simply did his job, but destroyed the incorrect building.

I know there were quite a few very upset people that day. The photo in the newspaper showed not just a pile of timber, but bits and pieces of tables, chairs, beds, books and many other items that had made the house into a home. Ordinary people do not set out to destroy their homes, nor do Christians take action to demolish their church buildings.

Today's readings speak of the destruction of an important building — the temple of the Lord! The Jews loved this building, because it was at the mercy seat in the 'Holy of Holies' that God met with his people. The temple was the centre of Jewish worship because it was there that the sacrifices were carried out. Those sacrifices pointed to the day when the Lord Jesus Christ would sacrifice himself for his people. The Jews would never have sent the bulldozers down to destroy that precious building.

Solomon's temple had been built to God's specifications and was loved by every citizen of Israel. God was pleased when his people obeyed and worshipped him as he had commanded. Our readings tell us of God destroying the temple that was so important in his worship. In verse 8 we read that God 'stretched out a line'. The plumb line was used by builders to ensure that the walls were upright and all was built correctly. However, God used the builder's line to ensure that the temple was totally destroyed. The plumb line would be used to ensure the building was levelled to the ground just as God had determined.

Jeremiah, the writer of Lamentations, wept with the godly people of Israel when they saw the building they loved as just a pile of rubble. Most of the people had been taken to Babylon as slaves and remained there for seventy years.

When the Lord Jesus told his disciples that the temple in which they had been standing would soon be destroyed they couldn't believe what they heard. However, in A. D. 70 the much loved building lay in ruins. God had deserted his people, because they had deserted him. The Jews had committed the most heinous sin possible. Peter told the Jews that they had 'taken by lawless hands ... crucified, and put to death' Jesus of Nazareth, God's only Son (Acts 2:23).

We all should remember that God hates sin and all sinners will be judged. Unrepentant sinners will be sent to hell for ever. God chastens his own people when they fall into sin, just as he did when the covenant people of Israel were sent into captivity and their centre of worship destroyed. God will have his people obedient!

If you love Jesus then you will show it by obeying his commands. May God bless all who love the Lord Jesus, and if you are not a Christian, pray that God will show you your sinful ways and turn you to Christ who is the only way of salvation.

> By the rivers of Babylon,
> There we sat down, yea, we wept
> When we remembered Zion.
> We hung our harps
> Upon the willows in the midst of it...
> Remember, O LORD, against the sons of Edom
> The day of Jerusalem,
> Who said, 'Raze it, raze it,
> To its very foundation!'

(Psalm 137:1,7).

To think about

1. Who was the great king of Babylon who overthrew Judah?
2. Why was the temple so important to the Jewish people?
3. In Psalm 137 the Jews were asked to sing a song of Zion. Why do you think the Babylonians would make such a demand of the captive Jews?
4. Why was Jerusalem overthrown in A. D. 70?

The wrong false teeth

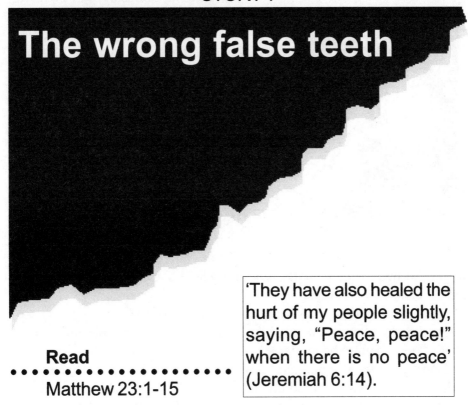

Read
● ● ● ● ● ● ● ● ● ● ● ● ● ● ● ● ● ● ●
Matthew 23:1-15

'They have also healed the hurt of my people slightly, saying, "Peace, peace!" when there is no peace' (Jeremiah 6:14).

When we are sick we visit a specialist who deals with diseases — a doctor. If I intend building a house I visit a specialist — an architect and a builder. If I need dental work done I visit a specialist — a dentist. If I am a sensible person I take notice of what the specialists tell me — after all, they are the ones who have studied their subject and know what they are doing.

If I need spiritual guidance I go to my Bible and if necessary ask a specialist to explain what the Scriptures teach — a minister of the gospel.

Today's text was of a time when God's people had turned their backs upon Jehovah and worshipped the gods of the surrounding nations. Many went through the motions of worshipping Jehovah, but there was no sincerity in their hearts. It was Jeremiah who warned the people of their impending overthrow because of their sinful ways. The ungodly Jews took no notice of his warnings, but went to the false prophets who said what they wanted to hear. These people said there was no danger of invasion by the Babylonians. Instead of war the Jews were to expect a period of peace. This made the people feel good. They could get on with their sinful lives and ignore the commands of Jehovah and the warnings of Jeremiah and the other faithful prophets. They thought they were going to the specialists who knew God's Word. However, their 'specialists' were in error!

31

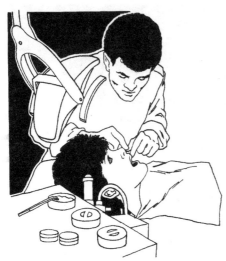

Other specialists are not without fault. Years ago a lady I know was on holiday. She had not taken care of her teeth when young and for years had worn a lower set of dentures. However, as they were wobbling in her mouth and needed relining, her husband suggested she visit a dental specialist and within a few days she would be smiling with a bright set of teeth.

She visited the dentist and for several days kept out of sight as she felt embarrassed without her teeth. Then came the phone call and she caught the bus to the dentist's surgery, where she was presented with a relined, cleaned lower plate.

'Put these in and pay as you go out,' said the dentist.

'But,' replied Samantha, 'they don't feel right. They wobble about in my mouth. They seem to be too large.'

'Don't you worry about that,' replied the dental specialist. 'In a couple of days they will have settled down and all will be fine. Do some reading aloud and that will help them settle into place.' Samantha paid the account, but the teeth began to hurt and on the bus home she sneaked them out of her mouth and put them in her handbag.

At home, when her husband saw her he burst out laughing and said, 'Those teeth look terrible. You look like a horse!' But Samantha persevered despite the fact that those who knew her pointed out that they couldn't possibly be her teeth.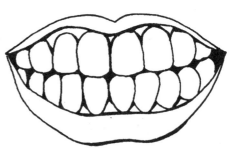

The next morning her husband drove her to the dental specialist. There he pointed to his wife and said, 'I didn't ask for a new wife. We just wanted the dentures repaired.'

The dentist looked at the teeth and then with an apologetic voice said, 'I'm so sorry, but you have the wrong dentures. I'll get yours.'

When he returned he was even more apologetic, 'I'm so sorry. Someone else was given your dentures and we're not sure who has them, but no one has returned to complain. I'll have to make you a new plate.'

At that point Samantha said, 'No! I'm going to someone who knows what they are doing!'

She then visited another dental specialist who did a perfect job and now she has a lovely smile and her dentures fit perfectly.

The Jews of Jeremiah's day were to find out that their 'specialist' prophets who pronounced, 'Peace, peace', when there was no sign of peace, were false. They didn't speak the words of God, but simply said what they knew the people wanted to hear. As a result the Lord warned them of punishment for their lies: 'Therefore they shall fall among those who fall… "I will surely consume them," says the LORD…' (Jeremiah 8:12-13). Later those prophets falsely prophesied safety for God's people: 'You shall not see the sword, nor shall you have famine, but I [the LORD] will give you assured peace in this place' (Jeremiah 14:13). These words must have been an encouragement to the people. It was just what they wanted to hear, but again the prophets told lies in the name of the Lord. God does not tolerate those who tell lies in his name and those who gave this false comfort to the people were warned: 'By sword and famine those prophets shall be consumed!' (Jeremiah 14:15). These false prophets seemed totally unashamed of what they said and had no fear of God who promised them punishment for their sinful activities.

The specialist dentist failed Samantha and throughout the ages men and women have led people astray in spiritual matters. Sometimes this has been done deliberately, while others sincerely believe what they are saying.

Today's reading contains Christ's condemnation of the scribes and Pharisees. They were the spiritual 'specialists', who led the people astray by teaching that salvation could be earned by obedience to God's law and the extra laws that they had added. Today we have the same problem where well-known 'ministers' have taught lies and led people astray.

We must all be on our guard in spiritual matters. A bad set of false teeth is a problem, but false doctrine can lead men and women to eternal hell. Nearly every person in the Western world has a Bible somewhere in their home. The Scriptures are the Word of God and must be used to check what pastors teach. We must all read our Bibles and know what they teach, otherwise we could be walking the broad way that leads to damnation.

A man or woman may be popular, praised by well-known, important people, pastor a big congregation, have their own radio or TV show, live in an upper-class suburb and carry and quote from a large, impressive Bible, but this is no guarantee that the message they preach is reliable.

May each one of our readers know Christ personally and be assured of their salvation.

> How sweet are your words to my taste,
> Sweeter than honey to my mouth!
> Through your precepts I get understanding;
> Therefore I hate every false way
>
> (Psalm 119:103-104).

To think about

1. How could you tell that a person is a false prophet?
2. Christ was a prophet. Why should we believe what he said?
3. Who were the Pharisees?
4. Who were the 'scribes'?

A faithful dog!

Read
• • • • • • • • • • • • • • • • •
2 Samuel 11:1-17

'Then Nathan said to David, "You are the man!"'
(2 Samuel 12:7).

How frightening it would be to have the police knock at your door and arrest you for a crime you had committed and thought no one knew anything about. Our text today contains the words of the prophet Nathan to King David who had committed some terrible sins and refused to acknowledge his guilt. God sent Nathan to him and after some time pointed the finger at the king and pronounced him guilty of adultery, murder and other sins: 'You are the man!'

One thing is certain as far as the ungodly are concerned — one day their

sins will be revealed. Their sins are sure to find them out (Numbers 32:23). They might successfully hide them from the sight of their family and friends, but God sees everything and no one can hide their sins from him.

Recently I read a humorous report in the newspaper of two thieves who went to great measures to hide their break and entry into a factory office. However, despite their careful planning, they overlooked their pet dog.

35

One of the thieves had been able to obtain the key to the office, where, the night before payday, a large sum of money was kept in a small safe. The plan was hatched to back a small truck up to the office door, unlock it and remove the safe. The thieves planned to open the safe when they returned to their garage. They were careful thieves — they wore masks to avoid recognition, and gloves so no fingerprints would be left.

Everything was well planned and the operation was carried out in what they believed to be a very successful way. After driving their small truck to

the factory, they soon had the safe on board and, laughing all the way home, drove into the garage, locked the door and went inside to have a cup of tea before starting work on the safe. They were so sure they had left nothing to chance, they were even planning how they would spend the thousands of dollars they were already calling their own.

Suddenly they heard some rather unexpected loud knocking on the door and, when one of the men looked through the window, he saw four police cars with armed police moving in to make an arrest. There was nothing they could do but open the door, and before long the police had the safe back where it belonged.

'But, how did you know it was us?' the thieves asked in amazement.

The answer was very simple.
Their pet dog loved to ride on the back of the truck and when the thieves left for the factory, unbeknown to them, he jumped on board. When they arrived he jumped off without the thieves noticing. While they were working on the safe the dog had entered the factory and settled down for a sleep.

When the police arrived they found the dog and began to wonder... So they followed the dog home. He knew the way! The best-laid plans of the men came to nothing except a long jail sentence. The newspaper that reported the story didn't indicate what happened to the dog.

King David saw from his palace the beautiful Bathsheba who was the wife of Uriah, one of his best soldiers. Lust filled his heart and before long he had committed adultery. David tried to cover his sins, but Bathsheba was pregnant and his wickedness would become obvious. Then he gave orders for faithful Uriah to be placed in the fiercest part of the battle where he was killed. Now David could marry Bathsheba and no one would ever know what a terrible sin he had committed.

God sent the prophet Nathan to him, who, after telling a simple little story which infuriated King David, was able to say to his sovereign, 'You are the man! ... Why have you despised the commandment of the LORD, to do evil in his sight? You have killed Uriah the Hittite with the sword; you have taken his wife to be your wife...' (2 Samuel 12:7, 9).

People try to hide their sins, but God often brings them to light. He uses a variety of ways to convict his people of their wickedness, but whatever method is used we should praise him for it. When a sinner repents he turns from his sins and loves righteousness.

If our sins are not revealed in this life they will certainly be revealed on Judgement Day, when it will be too late for repentance and saving faith.

May our sins trouble us till we turn to the Lord Jesus for cleansing. We read the promise found in Scripture: 'If we confess our sins, he is faithful and just to forgive us our sins and to cleanse us from all unrighteousness' (1 John 1:9). With sins forgiven and a saving faith in Christ there will be peace in our heart because God is at peace with us.

Have mercy upon me, O God,
According to your lovingkindness;
According to the multitude of your tender mercies,
Blot out my transgressions.
Wash me thoroughly from my iniquity,
And cleanse me from my sin

(Psalm 51:1-2).

To think about

1. Who was Nathan?
2. Discuss the story Nathan told David and why it made David angry. (Read 2 Samuel 12:1-4.)
3. Why could Nathan say to David, 'You are the man!'?
4. In what way was David punished by God for his sin with Bathsheba?

Keep off the flowers!

Read
••••••••••••••••••••
1 Kings 3:5-15

'But seek first the kingdom of God and his righteousness, and all these things shall be added to you' (Matthew 6:33).

If God asked you what you wanted more than anything else in the whole wide world, what would be your request? I know people who would ask for a lottery win, an expensive car, an overseas trip, a big mansion, or a long healthy life. Our text teaches us that the most wonderful thing that any person could ever want is membership in the kingdom of God. For a person to make that request means they have their priorities right.

I know people whose life is sport, sport and more sport, and they have no thought for God and eternal matters. Others neglect their families and spend their time at work trying to gain promotion.

In my teenage years on the farm we often suffered from severe flooding. In a large country town nearby many lost their lives 'in the big flood of '55'. At home we had the 'flood boat', and Dad and I often had to row to homes and rescue the inhabitants. We often spent time saving cattle from the rising water, but human life always came first. Most people really appreciated what we were doing, as it meant many hours of hard work helping people move from their homes to safe, higher ground. Others were complainers who never seemed satisfied with the work we did.

On one occasion it was my Mum and brother John who were the last to be taken to high ground after Dad and I had moved several families to safety. The river that flowed through our farmlands had burst its banks and filthy, muddy water was roaring past homes washing away property. Our car went under and we had six feet of water in our home. It was heartbreaking to find our clothes and furniture ruined.

One family sent out an urgent appeal for help, so Dad and I set out, rowing to their home, which was surrounded by miles of floodwater. When we arrived with hands and arms aching after rowing several miles through swiftly moving water we found that the fence around the house was under water, except for the two posts holding the gate in place. The water was several feet deep in the house and a much higher flood than ever before was expected.

The people were overjoyed to see us arrive, and, at first, everything said was in praise, 'Oh, thanks for coming. We were afraid we'd have to spend the night in the house and the water is rising swiftly!'

When the boat was tied securely in place, Dad jumped into water up to his chest and began wading towards the house verandah.

Suddenly the house owners looked in horror at Dad and the lady exclaimed, 'Look where you're going! You're walking over our flower garden and our flowers will be ruined! Take a little more care!'

Dad looked down. All he could see was muddy water up to his chest!

'Whatever do you mean?' he asked. 'I can't even see the flowers. They've probably all been washed into the river by now. We're here to rescue you and all you're interested in are flowers four feet under water!'

The woman had her priorities all wrong. She was more concerned about her garden, four feet under water and destroyed by floodwater, than she was about the well-being of herself and her husband.

However, they were pleased to be soon in the boat and on their way to safety. That night a huge tree smashed into one wall and almost destroyed their house. I'm sure they were pleased to have been rescued and taken to a safe house on dry, high ground.

We all need to look at our priorities in life. When God asked Solomon, 'Ask! What shall I give you?' God could have given wealth, a mighty kingdom, a long, happy life — anything he wanted. But Solomon simply said, 'Therefore give to your servant an understanding heart to judge your people, that I may discern between good and evil' (1 Kings 3:9).

A rich young ruler went to Jesus and asked a question, the answer to which revealed that his priorities were out of order: 'Good Teacher, what shall I do to inherit eternal life?' (Luke 18:18). Christ's reply showed the way he really felt — he loved his money more than eternal life.

May we all say 'Amen' to Christ's words, 'But seek first the kingdom of God and his righteousness...' To be right with God and a member of his kingdom is the most important event that will ever take place in your life. Everything else fades into insignificance when compared to this great truth.

Remember your Creator before the silver cord is loosed,
Or the golden bowl is broken,
Or the pitcher shattered at the fountain,
Or the wheel broken at the well.
Then the dust will return to the earth as it was,
And the spirit will return to God who gave it.
'Vanity of vanities,' says the Preacher,
'All is vanity'

(Ecclesiastes 12:6-8).

To think about

1. What are we taught by the above words from Ecclesiastes?
2. What should be No. 1 in our lives? Read Question 1 in the *Shorter Catechism.*
3. What did God think about Solomon's choice when he was asked what he wanted before everything else?
4. If you were asked the same question, what would be your reply and why?

Teeth can tell a story

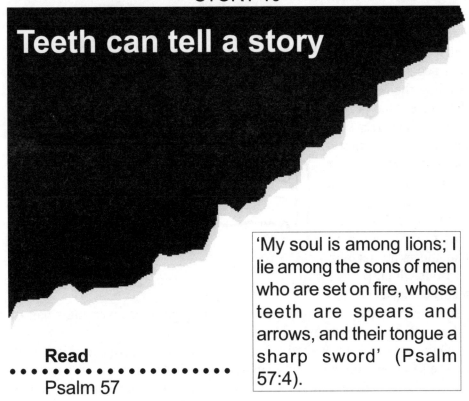

'My soul is among lions; I lie among the sons of men who are set on fire, whose teeth are spears and arrows, and their tongue a sharp sword' (Psalm 57:4).

Read
● ● ● ● ● ● ● ● ● ● ● ● ● ● ● ● ● ●
Psalm 57

In the New King James translation of the Scriptures the word 'teeth' appears forty-five times. Teeth add to our appearance and personality and often we can tell the character of a person simply by looking at his teeth — or lack of them! To meet a person who has a happy smile with their teeth clean and sparkling is a pleasant experience and usually marks a person out as being a kind, caring person.

Other people close their mouths and grind their teeth in anger. Before they speak we can tell they are going to be hurtful in what they say. Teeth play an important part in our life. I trust you look after yours! Remember these words: 'Be true to your teeth and they'll never be false to you!'

I have heard many funny stories about false teeth and have decided to tell you of one incident which was told me by a minister's wife who once worked in a hospital for the elderly. Each night she collected the patients' false teeth and carefully made sure they were in glass tumblers, correctly identified. In the morning, before returning them to their owners, she made sure they were well cleaned.

One morning when she was half way through the job she was called away. When she returned she continued handing them out, but discovered one person had no teeth. Her special glass was empty. During the time she was away, one lady had taken a second pair of teeth, but the problem was to discover who had the extra set and sort out which pair of teeth belonged to which

person, especially as most people were sitting up in bed wearing a pair of false teeth. However, someone had the wrong set!

Quickly she went from bed to bed and finally there sat one dear lady with two sets of upper dentures in her mouth. She smiled with a lovely smile of two rows of teeth and didn't want to hand them back. When she finally returned the extra pair of dentures the nurse had the job of sorting out which set of teeth belonged to which mouth. Many patients were very upset that morning, but finally, with kindness and love, everyone settled down, happy to be able to eat the food that came for breakfast.

In this psalm David cries out to God for help. King Saul was searching

for him to put him to death and he knew that his only hope was to be found in God. He was confident that God would save him from his enemies: 'He shall send from heaven and save me...' (v. 3). He knew he would be saved as God had promised that he would one day become king of Israel. He knew that God did not lie, but always fulfilled his promises.

Saul and the members of his army are described as having teeth like spears and arrows. The enemy 'gnashes at him with his teeth' (Psalm 37:12). The picture in Psalm 57 is of strong, sharp, canine teeth that animals use for tearing other animals apart before eating them. These type of teeth are fearful and describe what David's enemies would like to do to him. Like the canine teeth of wolves, lions and dingoes they held swords, spears and arrows ready to kill David as soon as they saw him. They spoke hateful words of the one God had appointed to be the future king of Israel. David saw their tongue as 'a sharp sword' (v. 4), but looked forward to the day when his enemies would be overthrown.

In Psalm 58:6 we read David's prayer: 'Break their teeth in their mouth, O God!' This was not a prayer that God would literally break the teeth of the enemy, but that God would prevent the spears and arrows of the enemy reaching their mark. In this way David would be saved from their anger.

Grinding or gnashing teeth are a sign of anger and distress, but there are several places where the expression is used to describe the feeling of those who are sentenced to eternal hell following Judgement Day. We read Christ's words in Matthew 25:30: 'And cast the unprofitable servant into the outer darkness. There will be weeping and gnashing of teeth.' On Judgement Day our expression will be either a smile of joy, love and gratitude towards God, or the grinding of teeth in remorse as we are cast into outer darkness.

> I will praise you, O Lord, among the peoples;
> I will sing to you among the nations.
> For your mercy reaches unto the heavens,
> And your truth unto the clouds.
> Be exalted, O God, above the heavens;
> Let your glory be above all the earth
>
> (Psalm 57:9-11).

To think about

1. Who in Genesis 49:12 is described as having 'teeth whiter than milk'?
2. We have an expression: 'I have escaped by the skin of my teeth.' Where in the Bible do we find this expression used? (Read Job 19.)
3. What does the above expression mean?
4. What does Psalm 57 teach us concerning God's care of his people?

A sad little dog!

Read
• • • • • • • • • • • • • • • • • • • •
Isaiah 42:1-9

'In that day the deaf shall hear the words of the book, and the eyes of the blind shall see out of obscurity and out of darkness' (Isaiah 29:18).

The Bible has many passages speaking about people who are both blind and deaf. Most of these passages refer to people who are spiritually deaf and blind, that is, they do not understand the wonderful truths of God's Word.

To be physically deaf and blind must be a real handicap. My Grandfather was totally deaf and this was a great problem for him. He was good at lip reading, but most of the time we had to write down what we wanted to say. At school I knew a young girl who was almost blind and life was extremely difficult for her.

A couple of years ago when Val and I were taking a holiday at the beach we saw a small dog wander into our garden. At first we didn't take much notice, but soon realized he had a problem. He was walking around in circles and often bumped into the fence. Then he'd turn away and before long bump into a tree trunk or get mixed up amongst the flowers. He was lost and had no idea where he was or where he was going.

I decided I should catch him and try and find if he had an owner. I wasn't keen on doing this as I thought he might bite me, so I took a towel to wrap him in. When I approached him I called gently, but he just kept walking about aimlessly.

I knew he was not well, so I picked him up in the towel and carried him to the garage where I had prepared some warm milk and dog food. His smell was very good as he immediately started drinking the milk and soon had everything eaten. Then he again started walking around aimlessly and I knew he was just an old dog who was both blind and deaf. Carefully I looked at the tag on his collar and there I saw a telephone number.

Soon an old man, who lived only several houses away, was on our doorstep. He had no idea that his dog had somehow escaped from the garden. When he saw his small, old dog he gently picked him up and said, 'Nicki, oh Nicki! What have you done?'

The dog knew who had picked him up, and he snuggled down into his owner's arms. After thanking us, the old man took his much loved dog home. He'd had Nicki since he was a pup and they really loved each other.

The man had been a doctor and now was living alone as his wife had died. Blind, deaf Nicki was his dear little friend and he didn't have the heart to have his 'mate' put down.

Unrepentant sinners are like that dog. They are both 'blind' and 'deaf' to the truths of God's Word. They can physically hear the words spoken by the pastor, but they can't understand the truth of those words. They read the words of Scripture and again they can't comprehend what is being said. To these people they just hear words.

The apostle Paul gives us the reason for this problem when he writes: 'But the natural man does not receive the things of the Spirit of God, for they are foolishness to him; nor can he know them, because they are spiritually discerned' (1 Corinthians 2:14). Yet when Christians hear the words of the Bible they love them and understand what is being taught because they have been born again by the Spirit of God. When Nicodemus visited Christ he was told of the necessity of being 'born again' (John 3:3) or he would never have a part in the kingdom of God. This means that spiritual eyes and ears need opening before we can be saved!

When Christ entered this world a wonderful work was carried out. We read in Isaiah 35:5: 'Then the eyes of the blind shall be opened, and the ears of the deaf shall be unstopped.' If you would be saved your eyes must be opened to spiritual truth.

Our text speaks of the problem faced by Israel. They had turned away from God and needed awakening. They needed spiritual surgery so they could hear the words of the 'book', the Bible. They also needed to be able to see in order to leave the world of darkness and sin and move into the light and liberty of God's truth.

Today, so many need the same spiritual surgery. May God be pleased to bless us with spiritual insight into the truth of his Word. May we all be enabled to hear God's call to repentance.

Poor little Nicki was both blind and deaf and nothing could ever be done to help him. If you are not a Christian there is nothing you can do to save yourself. You must see your sin and your need of a Saviour. When you begin to pray to Christ for salvation you should realize that the Holy Spirit is opening your spiritually blind eyes, unstopping your spiritually deaf ears and guiding you in prayer.

Salvation is all of God! May you know Christ as your Lord and Saviour. He came to set sin's prisoners free. May you know his salvation!

The LORD opens the eyes of the blind;
The LORD raises those who are bowed down;
The LORD loves the righteous.
The LORD watches over the strangers;
He relieves the fatherless and widow;
But the way of the wicked he turns upside down

(Psalm 146:8-9).

To think about

1. Read Matthew 13:13-15. What is Christ teaching in these few verses?
2. Of whom was the Lord speaking in Matthew 15:14?
3. Name one person who had their physical sight restored to them by Jesus. What was his response to the miracle? One such instance is found in John chapter 9.

Safe at last

'So the LORD saved Israel that day out of the hand of the Egyptians, and Israel saw the Egyptians dead on the seashore' (Exodus 14:30).

Read
• • • • • • • • • • • • • • • • • • • •
Exodus 14:8-31

Our text and reading are about God's marvellous work in saving his covenant people from Egypt. For many years they had served the Egyptians as slaves and life had become very difficult. They longed for the time when they would gain their freedom and be in the promised land — the land that flowed with milk and honey!

Our reading speaks of Israel at last obtaining their freedom. They were saved! However, salvation didn't mean they were safe in the promised land. They still had forty years of wandering in the desert before the children of

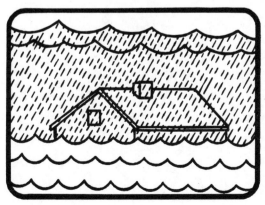

Israel could say, 'There in the distance we can see the land God promised Abraham. We are nearly home!'

In my childhood days our family lived on a farm. During those years we often suffered from severe flooding. Our house was built so that the flooring was about one and a half metres from ground level, which meant we usually didn't have water entering our house. The floor of our hay shed was also built up, which meant we could leave our car there, as well as other possessions.

One day rain began to fall and a flood was predicted, although not a big flood. The cattle were moved to high land, but we decided to leave the bull in his shed near the house. However, the rain kept falling and soon the bull

was standing in water. We moved him onto a loading ramp and gave him a bale of hay to eat — he had plenty of water to drink!

Two days later the water was up to his neck and the decision was made to rescue him. We rowed the boat to the ramp, put a rope around his neck and pushed him into the deep water. He started swimming, not knowing he had about a two-mile swim before he was safe on high dry land. I think he was like the Israelites leaving Egypt. They had a long, difficult journey before they reached Canaan.

So the bull swam and was pulled along behind the boat as Dad and I took turns rowing and holding the rope that was around the bull's neck. Several times he rolled over as if he'd had enough and was going to drown, but after a spell he struggled on. A couple of hours later the bull's feet touched ground. The water was still up around his shoulders and neck, but he didn't move. He was totally worn out! So there he stood for a quarter of an hour with head held high, breathing heavily.

He hadn't reached 'the promised land' yet, but soon he began moving towards the dry land. And at last, there he stood, high and dry with his head down chomping the grass. Now he had arrived, even though he was safe when his feet touched the ground. In fact, I felt sure he was going to reach safety from the very first step he made off the loading ramp into the deep water. He had us to keep him going and hold his head out of the water.

The Israelites were not safely home till they had crossed the Jordan River and had driven the inhabitants out of the 'promised land'. Then they would be able to settle down to a pleasant life. After walking out of Egypt they were saved, but faced difficult years before they were 'home'.

So it is with all who profess their faith in Christ. The day the Holy Spirit takes possession of our heart and we confess our love of the Lord Jesus we are saved, but we still have a long, difficult way to go before we reach the 'heavenly Jerusalem'.

If you have a saving faith in the Lord Jesus then show it by your faithfulness and courageous witnessing. Keep your eyes on the heavenly home he has promised all of his people. When we die we will pass into paradise. Even in death Christ is with his people. Nothing can separate us from the Lord who has saved us.

Paul put it like this: 'For I am persuaded that neither death nor life, nor angels nor principalities nor powers, nor things present nor things to come, nor height nor depth, nor any other created thing, shall be able to separate us from the love of God which is in Christ Jesus our Lord' (Romans 8:38-39).

Precious in the sight of the LORD is the death of his saints.
O LORD, truly I am your servant;
I am your servant, the son of your maidservant;
You have loosed my bonds.
I will offer to you the sacrifice of thanksgiving,
And will call upon the name of the LORD'

(Psalm 116:15-17).

To think about

1. Read Joshua 1:10-11. Describe the feelings of the people when they heard Joshua's commands.
2. What happens to a sinner at the moment he is saved?
3. Where is the repentant sinner's spiritual home? Read Hebrews 11:8-10.

A terrifying fall

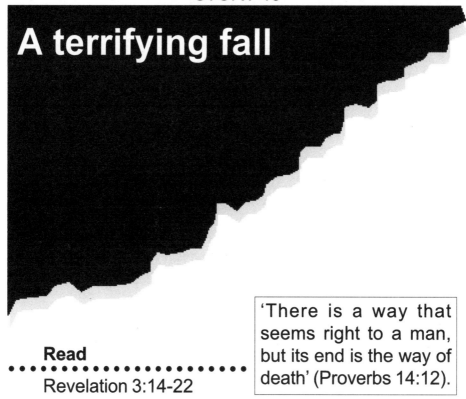

'There is a way that seems right to a man, but its end is the way of death' (Proverbs 14:12).

The book of Proverbs contains wise sayings that we should all live by, yet so many Christians ignore those precious words of Solomon.

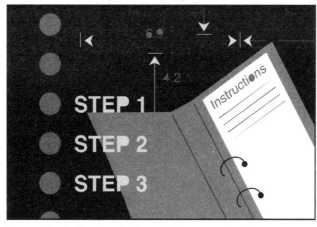

Most people frequently do things their own way because they believe they know best. Many times I have read the instructions indicating what should be done with some new piece of equipment, only to decide I could do it better my way, with the result that I needed assistance to undo my error.

Of course when we begin to follow our own plans the result is sometimes success, and even when we discover everything has gone wrong, it doesn't matter that much. But our text is very clear, for we are told that there is a way that seems right to us all, but the end result is death. Just ask some of your friends, who one day hope to reach heaven, what pathway they are following. The usual answer is that as long as they do their best God will open the gates of heaven and they will be welcomed in.

Not long ago I read of a family who visited an area where there is a very high waterfall. The area about the stream is fenced to prevent people doing anything foolish. When people want to cross the river they must walk along a bush track and over a bridge. That is the sure and safe way.

However, an accident was reported to the police because a person had been washed over the falls. The stream, about two yards in width, washed over the cliff face to the valley floor about one hundred yards beneath. A man decided that he would jump the river at that point instead of walking to the small bridge. No one was sure what happened next, but his plans misfired and he was swept over the cliff to his death. The man probably felt very secure in what he was doing and really believed he could make the jump without any difficulty. This story reminds me of our text: 'There is a way that seems right to a man, but its end is the way of death.'

In today's reading we are told of the situation in the church at Laodicea. The congregation felt that all was well. They did some good works and then believed that because of the riches that came their way, God was pleased with them. They said to one another: 'We are rich and have become wealthy. God has shown that he loves us. The way we live is the way to heaven.'

But Christ rejected such foolishness because he replied, 'You don't understand that really you are wretched, miserable, poor, blind and naked...' Our text applied to the Laodicean congregation: 'There is a way that seems right to a man, but its end is the way of death.'

Christ gave that congregation sound advice: 'I counsel you to buy from me gold refined in the fire, that you may be rich; and white garments, that you may be clothed, that the shame of your nakedness may not be revealed; and anoint your eyes with eye salve, that you may see...Therefore be zealous and repent' (Revelation 3:18-19). This alone was the way to heaven — repentance and a saving faith in Christ.

Today we must warn our ungodly friends and relatives that there is a way to heaven that seems perfectly right and proper to them — the way of good works and kindness — but the end of that way is death. No one has ever entered heaven by their own efforts, despite the encouraging words of the most knowledgeable people. We have heard it all: 'God loves everyone. Just do your best and one day you will find yourself in heaven.' This is not so and all who believe these enticing words will find out too late that it was a lie. The only way to heaven is through the works of another, the Lord Jesus. He, as the sinners' substitute, lived and died in their place. On the cross he died as sin-bearer and accepted the punishment due to his people for their sins. His work at Calvary put his people right with God. He perfectly obeyed God's law, and then gave to his believing people his own righteousness, which is our passport into the presence of God.

The only way to find the 'way' that is right with God is to turn to the Scriptures and read and pray that God will open the understanding of your heart — that the Holy Spirit might change you and give you a new heart filled with faith in Christ Jesus.

May you know the 'way' that leads to life and never follow that 'way' which leads to death. Remember that Jesus said, 'I am the way, the truth, and the life. No one comes to the Father except through me' (John 14:6).

Teach me your way, O LORD;
I will walk in your truth;
Unite my heart to fear your name.
I will praise you, O Lord my God, with all my heart,
And I will glorify your name for evermore

(Psalm 86:11-12).

To think about

1. What is the way into paradise? Read John 14:6.
2. List some 'ways' that other people think will put them right with God.
3. What was the 'way' the Pharisees believed would gain them a place in heaven?
4. Are you travelling the 'broad way' or the 'narrow way'? Read Matthew 7:13-14 and Luke 13:22-30.

Following Jesus

Read
• • • • • • • • • • • • • • • • •
1 Thessalonians 5:12-22

'Imitate me, just as I also imitate Christ' (1 Corinthians 11:1).

One morning at worship our pastor said, 'Obedience follows faith as surely as a trailer follows a car.' This is so true. Saving faith is always accompanied by the works of righteousness. The epistle of James puts it very clearly: 'For as the body without the spirit is dead, so faith without works is dead also' (James 2:26). Often we meet people who claim to be saved. 'Oh, yes,' they say, 'I'm trusting Christ as my Saviour, but not as my Lord.' They think they can be a Christian by saying the right words, yet continue living and loving sinful lives.

It is so true that a good trailer follows a car. One afternoon an elder, who was a student for the ministry, was driving me home from a worship service

in an outlying place when we saw a four-wheel drive vehicle coming rather quickly towards us. We noticed he was towing a trailer and even though it was still several hundred yards away from our car, we could tell something was wrong. The trailer was swerving from side to side and my friend, who was driving, said, 'Something's wrong! I'm going to slow down!'

Before we could do much, the trailer slipped sideways on the road and a wheel came off. The driver applied the brakes and his car and trailer sud-denly blocked our pathway, and my friend started to drive for a grassy strip beside the road. But a wheel was coming very quickly towards us, spinning and bouncing high. I just closed my eyes and ducked my head down as I thought the wheel would land on the bonnet and we'd end up in a smash. However, it bounced right over our car and into a drain. I looked up and breathed a sigh of relief to see the car and trailer coming to a stop in a shower of sparks from the trailer axle dragging on the roadway.

The trip home had been very frightening, but it proved that trailers are dangerous if they do not correct-

ly follow the car that pulls it along. So it is true that obedience is the consequence of saving faith. Anything less proves that the faith is not saving faith!

Christians are people who follow their Lord and Master. They imitate him in righteousness. The great apostle Paul, who faithfully followed Christ, could urge the Corinthian Christians to imitate his way of life, because he followed Christ.

The Scriptures have many commands for those who love the Lord Jesus. Today's reading is an outline for holy living. We are to 'pursue what is good both for yourselves and for all' (1 Thessalonians 5:15). Read the passage and make it your business to obey the instructions.

When Christ met Peter and Andrew, hard at work fishing, he said to them, 'Follow me, and I will make you fishers of men' (Matthew 4:19). Both men, we are told, did so 'immediately'. They were obedient to the command of their Lord and Saviour, Jesus Christ.

Christ commands every sinner who would follow him today: 'Whoever desires to come after me, let him deny himself, and take up his cross, and follow me' (Mark 8:34). To be a follower of Christ is not always an easy life. Each day we must take up our cross of faithfulness and serve the Lord Jesus. This way of life often causes difficulty for the Christian.

Today, in our part of the world, no one really cares much if we are Christians. However, in many countries, to follow Christ means carrying a cross, which sometimes leads to death. Every person who confesses to be a Christian must daily resolve to be willing to sacrifice everything they have for the Lord who loved them and saved them from their sins. The apostle Peter wrote, '…Christ also suffered for us, leaving us an example, that you should follow his steps' (1 Peter 2:21).

Your pastor and elders should be men who set a fine example of Christian living. The writer to the Hebrews wrote of those elders, 'Remember those who rule over you, who have spoken the word of God to you, whose faith follow…' (Hebrews 13:7).

While the trailer followed the car all was well, but as soon as it began to wobble about, trouble resulted. So also with Christians! As soon as we fail to follow Christ and fall into sin, we invite the chastening hand of God to bring us to repentance.

God's command to the Israelites applies to his people of all ages: '…what does the LORD your God require of you, but to fear the LORD your God, to walk in all his ways and to love him, to serve the LORD your God with all your heart and with all your soul, and to keep the commandments of the LORD and his statutes which I command you today for your good?' (Deuteronomy 10:12-13).

How can a young man cleanse his way?
By taking heed according to your word.
With my whole heart I have sought you;
Oh, let me not wander from your commandments!
Your word I have hidden in my heart,
That I might not sin against you!

(Psalm 119:9-11).

To think about

1. Name three people you admire and would like to imitate. What is there about them that you like?
2. What does your pastor mean when he calls upon you 'to follow Jesus'?
3. In the psalm portion above we read: 'Your word I have hidden in my heart.' What does this mean?

Pigs in the main street!

Read

Luke 15:11-24

The story of the 'prodigal son' is one of the best loved parables we find in the Bible. Amongst other truths it teaches us that we have a heavenly Father who is always ready to welcome home repentant sinners.

The story is of a young man who obtained his share of the inheritance and left home to have a great time in a city so far away that his father would never hear what he was doing. He wasted his money in sinful living and finally ended up in a sty caring for pigs.

What a humbling experience for that young Jew! Pigs were 'unclean' animals and I'm sure he would never have worked with them unless he had really reached the point where there was nothing else he could do in order to have food to live.

That young man wasn't satisfied with life at home. He wanted to try the bright lights and the big city. He was no different to so many young people today who are not happy living with their parents and can't wait to get away so they can do 'their own thing', only to discover the folly of their decision.

A farmer friend lived near a large country town, but there was a river between his farm and the bright lights of the town. He had a dozen or so pigs who must have listened to the noise that floated across the river from the township. During the evening the shining lights attracted their attention and put it into their piggy minds to visit the township across the river.

When the farmer was having his cup of tea after milking the cows he heard the radio announcer laughingly report that he'd received a phone call concerning half a dozen pigs trotting down the main street and suggested that if anyone owned them they should get them before they were run over and killed.

The farmer thought for a while, then decided he'd check on his pigs. He felt sure they couldn't be his as it would have meant a swim of fifty yards in running water to reach the town. To his surprise he discovered the sty gate was open and six of his pigs were missing. He just couldn't believe what had happened.

Wasting no time he climbed into his truck and set off over the bridge for the main street, but when he arrived, the pigs had disappeared. Soon he was amazed to see a crowd of people watching his six pigs swimming back across

the river towards their home. They were sick of the big town and knew where there was safety and food. The pigs had 'come to their senses' and gone home!

The wasteful son was in a pigsty when 'he came to himself' (v. 17). There he saw his sin — he had sinned against both God and his father. In the pigsty he repented of his sins and took the first step towards home. It was not just sufficient to repent, but he had to leave his evil friends and surroundings, confess his sin to his father and God, and beg their forgiveness.

We should all know well the story of the father looking down the roadway each day, with a hope in his heart that one day he would see his long gone son returning.

What a wonderful ending we find to this part of Christ's parable. There in the distance the father saw his son trudging along the road towards home. He ran to him, threw his arms around his neck and welcomed him home. He heard the sorrowful words of his son's repentance and the request that he be permitted to work on the farm just like his father's hired labourers.

But this young man was the son! It was still his home! His father was still his father! The father called for clothes and sandals, and ordered a servant to kill the fat calf because there was going to be a great welcome-home feast.

God, our heavenly Father, welcomes home all repentant sinners. The door to his kingdom is thrown open and after we are clothed in the righteousness of Christ we are escorted in to the sound of rejoicing angels and the welcome of the saints who have already reached their heavenly home. Christians should not want the things of the world, but be content with all that Christ has prepared for them.

If you are not a Christian, remember there is a heavenly Father who is ready to welcome you home if you come with a repentant heart, seeking forgiveness. The words of the apostle John should be of great encouragement to all sinners: 'If we confess our sins, he is faithful and just to forgive us our sins and to cleanse us from all unrighteousness' (1 John 1:9).

God's children should always rejoice because they have such a loving, caring, heavenly Father.

I acknowledge my sin to you,
And my iniquity I have not hidden.
I said, 'I will confess my transgressions to the LORD,'
And you forgave the iniquity of my sin

(Psalm 32:5).

To think about

1. There were two brothers in the parable. What did the elder brother think of the welcome that his father gave his wasteful son?
2. Why would it have been difficult for the son to work in a pigsty?
3. What is meant by 'forgiveness'?
4. Why does God forgive repentant sinners?

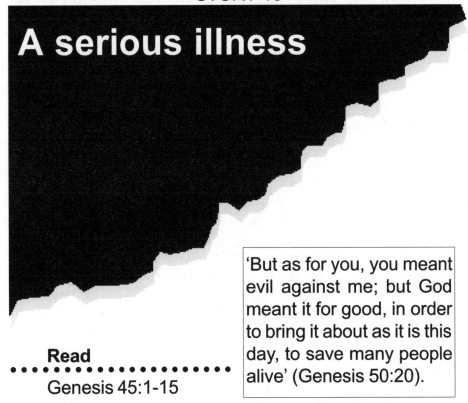

A serious illness

Read
• • • • • • • • • • • • • • • • •
Genesis 45:1-15

'But as for you, you meant evil against me; but God meant it for good, in order to bring it about as it is this day, to save many people alive' (Genesis 50:20).

There are times when it is difficult to believe the truth of the words of the apostle Paul when he wrote, 'And we know that all things work together for good to those who love God, to those who are the called according to his purpose' (Romans 8:28). God has a purpose in everything that happens — that he might be glorified and blessings flow to the saints. Sometimes these blessings are not seen in this life; but when Christians die they pass into the presence of God and enjoy all that Christ has prepared for them.

If ever a young man wondered what was happening to him it was Joseph. In his dreams he knew that God had a plan for his life, but when his brothers, out of hatred, sold him to some slave traders, he must have wondered if God's purposes for him were about to be undone. He was unjustly accused by Potiphar's wife and thrown into jail where he was confined for a long time. He went through some very trying times before he could see God's great purposes being fulfilled. Out of evil, good was to come.

A friend of mine suffered a serious kidney complaint which meant he had to be dialysed several times a week in a hospital well over a hundred miles away from his home. The doctor told him and his wife that if he did not receive a kidney transplant he would die. The man went through a long time of serious illness until the day arrived when the doctors found a kidney that was compatible with his body.

I visited him in hospital the day after his kidney operation and found him sitting up, smiling and eating a hearty meal. He had some setbacks, but it is now about twelve years since his operation and all is still going well.

However, out of that serious health problem, and all the difficulties his illness caused, the town in which he lives is now a better place. He and his wife realized that the town needed some dialysis equipment. For a sick person to travel over a hundred miles to a city centre three times a week was an added burden. The couple organized some good friends and interested citizens and they began to raise money for the establishment of a local dialysis centre. The work went on for years, but their hard toil and trouble paid off and today there is a special house fitted out with all the equipment needed to treat serious kidney complaints. No longer do locals have to travel great distances to have their blood cleansed. Out of a difficult, trying situation came good. The man's wife has recently been awarded the Order of Australia for all her hard work. She certainly deserved recognition for all she has done. If that man had not suffered that particular complaint, local people would still be driving many miles each week to receive life-saving treatment.

Joseph found himself in Egypt in jail. Yet when he interpreted Pharaoh's dreams he was released and given the job of preparing Egypt for the great drought which was to strike the land in seven years.

His brothers, who had sold him into slavery, were the very ones to benefit from the evil they had done. I always enjoy reading the story of Joseph dealing with his brothers so that they were brought to repentance for the evil they had done to him. He tricked them in such a way that they believed they would lose their lives. Shaking in fear they bowed down before him, just as he had dreamed many years before. Yet Joseph was a man of God who readily forgave them for their wickedness.

When the drought was most severe, Pharaoh invited Joseph's relatives to go to Egypt and live in Goshen. Their lives had been saved through the wickedness of his brothers. All that had happened turned out for good and Joseph was able to say, 'you meant evil against me; but God meant it for good, in order to … save many people alive'.

Evil men crucified the Son of God, the Lord Jesus Christ, yet out of that evil act repentant sinners are saved. Eternal life is ours through the sacrificial life and death of our Lord Jesus. The apostle Paul was locked up in a Roman prison, yet out of that difficult time the gospel was preached in Rome and many sinners were saved. Paul and Silas were whipped and thrown into jail at Philippi in order that a Philippian jailer might be saved. Our God rules the world for his own glory and the good of the saints. All things do work together for good and we should believe it!

King Nebuchadnezzar said of our all-wise and all-powerful God: 'All the inhabitants of the earth are reputed as nothing; he does according to his will in the army of heaven and among the inhabitants of the earth. No one can restrain his hand or say to him, "What have you done?" ' (Daniel 4:35).

When your world begins to fall apart, always remember that God is in control and out of your hard time good will come. You may not recognize what it is, but be assured that this is always the case. God is ever being glorified through the events of this world and the suffering of his people!

But as for me, I trust in you, O LORD;
I say, 'You are my God.'
My times are in your hand;
Deliver me from the hand of my enemies,
And from those who persecute me.
Make your face shine upon your servant;
Save me for your mercies' sake

(Psalm 31:14-16).

To think about

1. Who were Joseph's mother and father?
2. How many members of Joseph's family went to live in Egypt?
3. Where was Joseph buried?
4. Name four of Joseph's brothers.

The magpie that didn't forget

Read
• • • • • • • • • • • • • • • • • • •
Ecclesiastes 12:1-14

'Remember now your Creator in the days of your youth, before the difficult days come' (Ecclesiastes 12:1).

To remember your Creator is very good advice. To remember God while you are young is even better advice, because none of us know if we will reach old age or how long our brain will remember anything. 'Remember' is a very special word in my Bible, in fact it is found 164 times.

During our life many things happen which we remember with joy. Of course there are events we wish we could forget. Most of you who read my books were taught the truth about God when you were young and I trust you remember what you were taught about almighty God who created this great universe.

I'd like to tell you a true story about a bird, a magpie, who never forgot the man who befriended him when he was injured. A man was driving his car along a bush road when he spied a baby magpie flapping about on the side of the road. Realizing the bird couldn't fly he stopped and, after some chasing, finally managed to catch it. The dear little bird lay on his big hand and it

was then that the man realized that it had a broken wing. It had most likely been struck by a passing vehicle.

Feeling sorry for the little bird he wrapped him up in his jacket and, after a visit to a veterinary surgeon, took him home. He cared for that magpie which, because of its broken wing, was never to fly again. The man fed the bird and kept the family cat out of the way. After a while the magpie had 'the run of the house' and the cat took no notice of the magpie, which had a sharp beak and quite strong claws. Often the bird would flap his way onto the man's shoulder and sit there for hours making warbling noises in his ear. The man and the magpie became very close friends for several years.

When the family moved into New South Wales from their home state of Victoria they were told the law prevented them having a wild animal as a pet. After some heartache the magpie was given to a naturalist who had a huge aviary for birds unable to survive in the wild. But Victorian magpies never forget.

Several years later the man was passing the aviary and called in to see his magpie friend. The wildlife officer was just about to feed the birds so he told the man to enter the aviary through a door about fifty metres from where the feeding was taking place. He was told to step inside and stand there without making a noise. They would then see what the magpie would do.

All the birds were pecking at their food when the magpie saw his long-lost friend in the distance. He stopped eating, fluttered into the air and glided till he landed on his human friend's shoulder, where he started to warble in the man's ear, just as he had done many years before. He had not forgotten the man who befriended him when he was just a small, injured bird.

Together the man sat with his magpie friend and for a time they just looked at one another. He stroked his bird friend as the tears came into his eyes. The magpie still remembered him, despite the fact they had not seen one another for over two years.

What a wonderful thing it is to remember those important truths we were taught in our youth. In this book of the Bible, Solomon reminds all young people to 'Remember now your Creator in the days of your youth.' Today, remember God

who created this universe, because the day might come when you are so involved in other time-consuming activities that you have no time to remember your Creator. I was once asked to visit an elderly lady who was in hospital. I did not know the woman, but one of her friends was concerned about her well-being and asked me to speak to her dear companion. When I arrived, I discovered that she was connected to much hospital equipment, and was so ill that it was not possible to hold a conversation with her. She was not a Christian and her 'difficult days' had come. She was more concerned with her medical treatment than her spiritual need of Christ. As she groaned in pain I read a short passage of the Scriptures and prayed that God would bless her both spiritually and physically. However, sadly, I left her bedside with the impression that my visit had come too late.

If you are past the age of being young, Solomon has another 'remember' for you: 'Remember your Creator before the silver cord is loosed, or the golden bowl is broken…Then the dust will return to the earth as it was, and the spirit will return to God who gave it' (Ecclesiastes 12:6-7). Here Solomon is giving some good advice to all of us: remember your God before you die. A Christian once said, 'When it is time for you to die, make sure that all you have to do is die.' This will be so if you are a Christian and living at peace with God. And the one way to 'remember' your God is to become friends with him through faith in his Son, the Lord Jesus Christ.

Jesus Christ is the sinners' Saviour. He alone can save sinners and the psalmist invites you to 'Kiss the Son, lest he be angry, and you perish in the way, when his wrath is kindled but a little' (Psalm 2:12).

Christians remember their Redeemer in special ways. Every Sunday is a reminder that Christ rose from the dead on the first day of the week. We remember the saving death of the Lord Jesus when we sit at the Lord's table with like-minded Christians and eat the bread and drink the wine, which is a reminder of his broken body and shed blood.

We remember our God by reading the Scriptures, by going to him in prayer, by reading good Christian books and mixing with his people. May God bless you and may you all, 'Remember your Creator in the days of your youth, before the difficult days come' (Ecclesiastes 12:1).

I will remember the works of the LORD;
Surely I will remember your wonders of old.
I will also meditate on all your work,
And talk of your deeds

(Psalm 77:11-12).

To think about

1. Who was Solomon?
2. Why did Solomon give the advice: 'Remember now your Creator in the days of your youth, before the difficult days come'?
3. Why should people be concerned about God when they are young? Isn't that the time to enjoy yourself in the world?
4. See if you can find another place in the Bible where the word 'remember' is found. Discuss that passage.

A slight boating accident!

Read
• • • • • • • • • • • • • • • • • • •
Luke 12:13-21

'Come now, you who say, "Today or tomorrow we will go to such and such a city, spend a year there, buy and sell, and make a profit"; whereas you do not know what will happen to-morrow' (James 4:13-14).

I'm sure there are days when we wonder how the weather forecasters make their predictions. Sometimes I think they look at the sky during the afternoon and make their prediction on the basis of each day being very much alike. Rain today and the chance of rain tomorrow; fine today and probably fine tomorrow. Isaiah wrote of Israel's ungodly, drunken rulers who thought their drunken parties would go on from day to day: ' "Come," one says, "I will bring wine, and we will fill ourselves with intoxicating drink; tomorrow will be as today..." ' (Isaiah 56:12). What they thought were good days, suddenly came to an end when God's judgement fell. None of us know with assurance what tomorrow holds for us! We cannot be sure what will happen in the next hour.

Today's reading is of a rich man who made all the necessary plans so he could sit back and enjoy his retirement. However, he didn't count on God bringing his life to a sudden end!

I trust you can enjoy the picture included in this story. It was taken in June 1932 when cameras were not of the same quality as they are today. However, it caught people in a situation that was unexpected. The photo and story appeared in a local paper and finally ended up in the *New York Times* as being one of the finest news pictures of that time.

A boat load of people were to travel up a river and then enjoy an overland journey to the wharf where they would board the boat to take them back to Newcastle in New South Wales, Australia. A reporter, Jack Little, decided to stay with the boat and, as it approached the wharf to load the passengers after their bus trip, he prepared his camera to capture the excitement, little realizing that the wharf was about to collapse under the weight of the crowd.

He aimed his camera at the excited, chattering crowd, who expected to board the boat and complete their journey, when without warning the wharf

gave way. Well-dressed men and women slid into the water and if you look carefully you can see a man clinging to the top of a pole, thrown there by the falling wharf.

Those people suddenly found their plans ruined. The totally unexpected had happened. When Jack Little had his photograph developed he realized he had a great picture.

In our parable the rich man found the unexpected happened. Instead of sitting back and enjoying the fruits of his labour he was standing before the judgement seat. Instead of joy, total horror!

In his epistle, James warned his Jewish readers that they could never be sure of what the future held for them. The Jews were known as energetic traders who made careful plans to travel to distant places to buy and sell and make money. However, they had no control over the future. None could be sure whether the next morning they would be alive or in the grave.

We need to be conscious of this truth, but Christians can also rest easy because our God controls the future. Not even the little sparrow dies without God having planned it that way. God even knows the number of hairs on our head. He controls every aspect of human history.

While we don't know what the future holds, and we make our plans for the future, we can be sure of this truth: 'And we know that all things work together for good to those who love God, to those who are the called according to his purpose' (Romans 8:28).

> LORD, make me to know my end,
> And what is the measure of my days,
> That I may know how frail I am.
> Indeed, you have made my days as handbreadths,
> And my age is as nothing before you;
> Certainly every man at his best state is but vapour.
> Surely every man walks about like a shadow;
> Surely they busy themselves in vain;
> He heaps up riches,
> And does not know who will gather them
>
> (Psalm 39:4-6).

To think about

1. Discuss some plans you made that came to nothing.
2. Who controls your future on the human level and over all?
3. If God controls the future, do you think we should make any plans? Why?
4. What is taught in today's psalm portion?

He missed his surprise party

Read
2 Peter 3:1-13

‘For you yourselves know perfectly that the day of the Lord so comes as a thief in the night’ (1 Thessalonians 5:2).

The Scriptures have a lot to say about the second coming of the Lord Jesus. The word 'sudden' is often used to describe that event because none of us know the day when the Lord will return. It will be sudden and, for most people, unexpected. Some will be going about their business, marriages will be taking place, others will be enjoying their hobbies and many will be sound asleep, when the heavens part and Christ appears accompanied by the host of angels and the souls of the departed saints.

No one will miss out on the event as we are told in Revelation 1:7: 'Behold, he is coming with clouds, and every eye will see him, even they who pierced him.' God has planned that day perfectly and none will miss the occasion.

When people make their plans, so often something is forgotten. My brother John had decided to enter the ministry and had sent his resignation to the Department of Education. The teachers at his school decided to give him a farewell lunch on his last school day. It was to be a

surprise for John and everyone was sworn to secrecy. The last school day arrived, the food was prepared and during the morning some ladies prepared the hall with decorations, tables, chairs and food in plenty. At the morning recess John was somehow kept away from the hall as this was to be a big surprise farewell for him.

About five minutes before the lunch bell indicating lunchtime was over and it was time to return to school, John returned from a short walk down town, to be met by a rather upset group of teachers who said, 'Where have you been? You missed your party and all the food has been eaten!'

All John could reply was, 'No one told me.'

I'm sure that when Christ returns to this earth there will be many who will say of his coming, 'No one told me!' However, you will not be able to say that. Today many people mock Christians because of their firmly held belief of Christ's return, but the day is coming when everyone will bow their knee to the Lord Jesus and confess that he is the Lord of glory, whether they once believed it or not (Philippians 2:10-11).

Every person, from Adam to the last baby born before Christ returns, will see his appearing in power and glory. For the faithful Christians it will be a wonderful day because the curse of sin will have gone for ever. The saints will rise from their graves and with the glorified, living saints, rise to meet the Lord in the air (1 Thessalonians 4:14-17). The ungodly will also rise to a judgement of condemnation, to be separated from all that is good — to spend eternity in hell!

That day will be one of terror for unrepentant sinners, especially those who knew the truth and turned their back upon the salvation freely offered. Paul wrote of their terrible day: 'when the Lord Jesus is revealed from heaven with his mighty angels, in flaming fire taking vengeance on those who do not know God, and on those who do not obey the gospel of our Lord Jesus Christ' (2 Thessalonians 1:7-8).

John missed out on his surprise party, but sinners will not miss out on the surprise of the ages on that day! All who read these pages should take note of the invitation given by God and recorded in Isaiah 55:1, 3: 'Ho! Everyone who thirsts, come to the waters; and you who have no money, come, buy and eat. Yes, come, buy wine and milk without money and without price... Incline your ear, and come to me. Hear, and your soul shall live.'

> Lift up your heads, O you gates!
> Lift up, you everlasting doors!
> And the King of glory shall come in.
> Who is this King of glory?
> The LORD of hosts,
> He is the King of glory

(Psalm 24:9-10).

To think about

1. What makes a surprise party a success?
2. Who is 'the King of glory' spoken of in the psalm portion above?
3. What will happen to the bodies of those who are dead when the Lord returns? Read 1 Corinthians 15:51-54.
4. Who knows the date and time of Christ's return? Read Matthew 24:36.

I couldn't do it

'Then he will also say to those on the left hand, "Depart from me, you cursed, into the everlasting fire prepared for the devil and his angels ..."' (Matthew 25:41).

Read
• • • • • • • • • • • • • • • • • • • •
Revelation 20:11-15

In our modern, western world most people believe there are two things that matter: authority and power. Humans respect people who have the authority to issue orders and the power to carry them out. Authority is often accompanied by wealth, and a gun that ensures obedience!

Mum and Dad give orders and they should be obeyed, not because they hold a big stick, or promise a bribe for obedience, but simply because we love them. Some people have authority to issue commands, but don't have the power to ensure they are carried out, while others have great power but

don't use that power to make their wishes come to pass.

Funerals are sad occasions because they remind us of the wages of sin and that one day we all part from our loved ones. Even though the one whose body is being laid to rest is a Christian and with his Lord and Saviour, the funeral is still a time of sorrow. The minister conducting the service always wants things to go well and is very careful with the organization. I always made it my habit to ask the mourners whether they wanted the coffin at ground level or already lowered into the grave before they reached the graveside. Some people find it very stressful to see

a loved one lowered into the earth and prefer to gather beside a grave where the coffin is not visible.

On one occasion a distressed wife asked for the coffin to be lowered before the mourners arrived. As I arrived at the graveside first I gave the instruction to lower the coffin at once. I had the right to make the request, but very soon discovered I had no power to see my order carried out. The gravediggers had done a bad job with the grave — it wasn't long enough for the coffin to fit!

I said, 'Please try!' However, I was asking the impossible. I apologized to the upset woman and the rest of the service went as planned. Later I asked the undertaker if this happened very often and was told that it happened occasionally. I had the authority, but lacked the power to carry out my request.

One day an angry man shouted out at me, 'Go to hell!' I smiled inwardly as I knew he lacked both the authority to say such a thing and the power to carry it out. However, this is not so with the Lord Jesus. On Judgement Day he will order the ungodly into hell. Sin has offended God and he has authority and power to carry out his judgements.

In Psalm 2 we read of people and nations raising their fists at God and declaring they will not be bound by his law. However, the psalmist tells us that God has appointed his Son as King of the universe, and he will use his almighty power to overthrow his enemies. We read, 'You shall break them with a rod of iron; you shall dash them to pieces like a potter's vessel' (Psalm 2:9). Jesus Christ was given all authority in heaven and on earth (Matthew 28:18) and he has the power to carry out all his purposes.

One day, as surely as you read these words, you will face the Son of God who is the judge of all mankind. I urge you all to make peace with God before that day, for the psalmist says, 'Kiss the Son, lest he be angry, and you perish in the way, when his wrath is kindled but a little. Blessed are all those who put their trust in him' (Psalm 2:12).

Let the heavens rejoice, and let the earth be glad;
Let the sea roar, and all its fullness;
Let the field be joyful, and all that is in it.
Then all the trees of the woods will rejoice before the LORD.
For he is coming, for he is coming to judge the earth.
He will judge the world with righteousness,
And the peoples with his truth

(Psalm 96:11-13).

To think about

1. By what standard will God judge the world?
2. List five examples of God's great power.
3. List three examples of God declaring he would do something and then carrying it out.
4. Talk about something you would like to do, but don't have the power to bring it to pass.

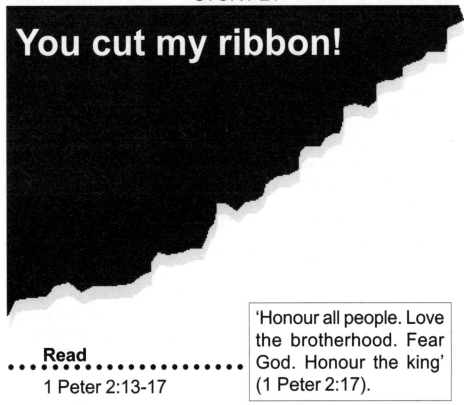

You cut my ribbon!

Read

1 Peter 2:13-17

'Honour all people. Love the brotherhood. Fear God. Honour the king' (1 Peter 2:17).

The Scriptures contain commands to honour our rulers, yet many people spend a lot of time criticizing the political rulers God has placed over them. In our democracies we elect our politicians, yet very few people acknowledge that those elected are in their positions of power because God has decreed it to be so.

The great King Nebuchadnezzar acknowledged the kingship of God when he wrote: '…the Most High rules in the kingdom of men, gives it to whomever he will, and sets over it the lowest of men' (Daniel 4:17). Jeremiah records the words of the Lord where he declares that God gave the kingdom of Babylon to Nebuchadnezzar (Jeremiah 27:5-7). Yes, it is God who 'removes kings and raises up kings' (Daniel 2:21).

We are commanded to honour those who rule over us. When the apostle Paul was asked how the Roman Christians should cope with living in pagan Rome, they were told to obey the government: 'Let every soul be subject to the governing authorities' (Romans 13:1).

On Saturday 19 March 1932 Sydney Harbour Bridge was ready for its great opening ceremony. The bands had practised their music, soldiers were to be there, dressed in their finest uniforms, and Mr Jack Lang, the Premier of New South Wales, and politicians of all parties were invited to be present when the Premier, with his golden pair of scissors, would cut the ribbon and allow citizens to cross the bridge for the first time.

But it was depression days and in political circles feelings ran high. Mr Lang was not well liked by many people. One man, Captain Francis De Groot, a member of an anti-government group called the New Guard Movement, had no respect for Mr Lang and the policies of his party, and had decided to shame him by preventing him from being the one to cut the ribbon at the official occasion. Dressed in

his army clothing, and riding a fine-looking horse, he was able to make his way quite close to the official party. The police and other officials thought he was one of the honour guard. After all the speeches were finished, Mr Lang stepped forward with his scissors and just as he was about to cut the ribbon and declare the Sydney Harbour Bridge open, Captain De Groot spurred his horse forward and with sword raised high charged the ribbon and slashed it in half.

This was De Groot's great act of disobedience — he humiliated the Premier he despised. He didn't honour his political rulers. Captain De Groot was quickly dragged from his horse and taken to the asylum where he spent several days before being fined and released. At the bridge the ribbon was quickly joined and Mr Lang finally cut it a second time, declaring the Sydney Harbour Bridge officially open.

Many people considered De Groot's action to be a great joke while others found his behaviour very embarrassing and demeaning. What he did was a deliberate act of disobedience to the law of the land.

If people do not obey the law, society falls apart. Even the wicked Roman government was to be obeyed unless its laws contravened God's Word. It was appointed by God for the good of society. Even a bad government is better than no government at all. Paul reminded his Roman Christians that if they obeyed the law they would have nothing to fear. They were also to pay their taxes. Paul concluded: 'Render therefore to all their due: taxes to whom taxes are due, customs to whom customs, fear to whom fear, honour to whom honour' (Romans 13:7).

We must always remember that God rules this world, not our politicians. In Proverbs 8:15 we read: 'By me kings reign, and rulers decree justice...' And when decisions are made by our rulers remember that it is God who causes such decisions: 'The king's heart is in the hand of the LORD, like the rivers of water; he turns it wherever he wishes' (Proverbs 21:1).

May all Christians be known as people who submit to the government for the sake of the Lord (1 Peter 2:13). May we be the best citizens in our land, but when there is a problem concerning the law of God and the law of the land it is God's law that must be obeyed, just as the apostle Peter said, 'We ought to obey God rather than men' (Acts 5:29).

'I will declare the decree:
The LORD has said to me,
"You are my Son,
Today I have begotten you.
Ask of me, and I will give you
The nations for your inheritance,
And the ends of the earth for your possession.
You shall break them with a rod of iron;
You shall dash them to pieces like a potter's vessel"'

(Psalm 2:7-9).

To think about

1. Who is head of your government?
2. How can you show respect for those in positions of leadership?
3. What are you to do if your government suddenly greatly increases taxes to be paid?
4. What is the best you can do for your rulers?

Don't wreck the garage, please!

Read
• • • • • • • • • • • • • • • • • •
Ephesians 2:19-22

'...you also, as living stones, are being built up a spiritual house, a holy priesthood, to offer up spiritual sacrifices acceptable to God through Jesus Christ' (1 Peter 2:5).

Most people live in houses, but the types of houses throughout the world differ greatly. In the Pacific Ocean region they are largely built of bamboo and grass. Eskimos build their homes from blocks of ice. Most western countries use the readily available material, so we find that timber and bricks are widely used. Some people in our region make mud-brick homes that are very suitable for the climate.

Whatever is used, the material has to be solidly put together. We find that nails are ideal for timber. Bricks are cemented into place and where bamboo and grasses are used the material is woven. Of course the building must have a solid foundation or it would soon collapse.

As well as houses there are many other types of buildings: halls, church buildings, shops, factories, cubby-houses and other structures. There is one great building that is largely unseen by the world and that is the temple of the Lord. It is not built of bricks, stones or timber, but people. Our reading indicates that the saints are the building material of God's temple, built on the foundation of the apostles and prophets, and having a beautiful corner-stone, the Lord Jesus Christ. This building cannot be destroyed.

Some time ago we built our first home and the builder used bricks; but as our finances were limited we could only put down the cement slab for the garage. When we had the money the builder returned to complete the work. He had finished the brick walls and decided to do another job, but promised to return in a couple of weeks. Each day we parked the car on the unfinished garage floor, but the children usually wanted it out of the way so they could play on the cement.

One day, when they asked their mother if she would mind moving the car, they helped her push it in order to save her going into the house to get the keys. Val's plan was to have the door open and when the car was moving sufficiently she would jump into the seat and steer the car out of the way. However, her plan didn't work. She jumped into the car but was too slow closing the door.

The car door struck the brick wall. Suddenly there was a crashing sound and there beside the car lay part of the wall. About two hundred bricks had been torn out of the wall. The car wasn't damaged, but Val was rather upset.

Daily we hear of our buildings falling down in storms, cyclones, earthquakes and violent winds. However, that is not so concerning the temple that Christ is constructing. His building cannot be destroyed. The disciple Peter had just made a wonderful confession concerning Christ: 'You are the Christ, the Son of the living God,' to which Jesus replied, 'Blessed are you, Simon Bar-Jonah, for flesh and blood has not revealed this to you, but my Father who is in heaven. And I also say to you that you are Peter, and on this rock I will build my church, and the gates of Hades shall not prevail against it' (Matthew 16:16-18).

The foundation of God's temple is the Lord Jesus Christ, the Son of the living God. This is a great truth, which is believed by each person who forms a part of that temple. Paul wrote: 'For no other foundation can anyone lay than that which is laid, which is Jesus Christ' (1 Corinthians 3:11).

Our buildings will eventually all fall down and be obliterated, but Christ's temple (his people) will last for ever. It is the new Jerusalem which one day will inherit the new heavens and new earth. (Read Revelation 21:9-21.) Every brick in God's temple is bound together by love of God and love of one another — a love which cannot be destroyed. We are all indwelt by the Holy Spirit, all have a living faith in Christ and all have a common destiny: being in the presence of God.

Good things are in store for the saints. May God bless you with a living faith in Christ so you can take your place in God's spiritual temple and then with all the saints offer perfect spiritual sacrifices to God through Christ.

The stone which the builders rejected
Has become the chief cornerstone.
This was the LORD's doing;
It is marvellous in our eyes.
This is the day the LORD has made;
We will rejoice and be glad in it

(Psalm 118:22-24).

To think about

1. What holds your house together?
2. What makes your house into a home?
3. What 'spiritual sacrifices' can you offer to God? Read Hebrews 13:15.
4. What use is a 'cornerstone'? Why is Christ the best 'cornerstone' for God's temple?

Enjoy your swim!

Read

• • • • • • • • • • • • • • • • • • •

Isaiah 55:1-7

'Call upon me in the day of trouble; I will deliver you, and you shall glorify me' (Psalm 50:15).

Australia is an island nation completely surrounded by water. Our seasons are very pleasant, so the beaches are very popular in the warmer months. Each summer weekend the roads are crowded with cars taking their occupants to the ocean to enjoy a time in the surf. Securely tied to the roof racks you will notice brightly coloured surfboards, ready for shooting the waves,

for 'hanging five', and if they are really competent, 'hanging ten'.

I used to enjoy body surfing, but have always wished I had tried the surfboard, as riding the waves seems an exciting sport. Val and I and our girls spent many happy hours on Australian beaches. Before we were married Val and I attended a teachers' college situated near the ocean and we often spent a hot afternoon in the cool ocean breakers.

The most popular beaches are patrolled by surf lifesavers — men and women who have sacrificed much of their time caring for swimmers who get into trouble. Often rips develop which drag unsuspecting swimmers out to sea.

81

Usually these people panic and try to swim to shore against the moving water, only to tire and in some cases drown. Sensible swimmers know that it is best to swim across the rip and, when out of the current, to shoot the waves to the shore. If the situation gets desperate the surfer in difficulty is supposed to raise his hand, wave and call out for help.

The lifesavers soon come to the rescue as they sit in towers keeping a watch out for swimmers in difficulty, and for the sharks that sometimes cruise near the shore.

On one occasion when Val found herself in very deep water, she forgot to swim for the shore, but in panic grabbed me and climbed up till she was standing on my shoulders with her head out of water. I sank to the sand beneath and felt sure I was going to drown. However, God was good, and we both made it to the shore. Val has never since tried to drown me like that!

When swimmers find themselves in a drowning situation there is usually little they can do. They panic, begin to breathe the salty water into their lungs and then slowly sink below the surface.

When sinners are awakened to their need of salvation they also discover they can do nothing to wash away their sins or earn forgiveness.

Without Christ they begin to sink under the weight of their sins. They can cry for help and God has given sinners a promise which we read in our text: 'Call upon me in the day of trouble; I will deliver you, and you shall glorify me' (Psalm 50:15).

The words of Isaiah 55:6-7 should bring comfort to all under conviction of sin: 'Seek the LORD while he may be found, call upon him while he is near. Let the wicked forsake his way, and the unrighteous man his thoughts; and let him return to the LORD, and he will have mercy on him; and to our God, for he will abundantly pardon.'

We have a command and a promise: 'Believe on the Lord Jesus Christ, and you will be saved...' (Acts 16:31). The Lord Jesus delights to save sinners and God has no pleasure in the death of the wicked. What we could not do, Christ has done in his life and death. All who trust in him for salvation have their sins forgiven and are covered with his righteousness.

Jesus is our lifesaver! Doing good deeds can't save, being a nice person won't save you, nor can following the teaching of the 'wise men' of the eastern religions. Again in the book of Acts we read Peter's words, 'Nor is there salvation in any other, for there is no other name under heaven given among men by which we must be saved' (Acts 4:12).

When you have been given a saving faith in Christ, you will produce evidence of your salvation — you will obey the commandments of God. Every time I visit the beach and see the lifesavers on duty I am reminded of the 'Lifesaver' of my soul — the Lord Jesus Christ. May he be your 'Lifesaver' too!

Let all those who seek you rejoice and be glad in you;
And let those who love your salvation say continually,
'Let God be magnified!'
But I am poor and needy;
Make haste to me, O God!
You are my help and deliverer;
O LORD, do not delay

(Psalm 70:4-5).

To think about

1. Who is the only one who can save sinners?
2. What did he do to bring about the salvation of sinners?
3. What does the name Jesus mean? Read Matthew 1:21.
4. What promise was given by God in Genesis 3:15? How was it fulfilled?

You didn't listen!

Read
• •
Hebrews 1:1-14

'No prophecy of Scripture is of any private interpretation [origin], for prophecy never came by the will of man, but holy men of God spoke as they were moved by the Holy Spirit' (2 Peter 1:20-21).

I'm sure that many of my readers have heard professing Christians make the claim when they are about to start something new in their life, 'God told me to do this,' or 'God revealed this to me.' When people say this to me I usually ask the person, 'How did God tell you? Did he write it on the wall?'

While I ask this question, I know that God does still speak, but usually people don't bother to listen. When I say, 'God speaks to me,' you should immediately ask me, 'How does God speak to you?'

Some time ago I heard of a young girl who wanted to go to her friend's place for an afternoon of games. Her mother didn't want her to go and told her that instead she could make herself busy around the house. The child wasn't happy with her mother's reply and spent some time complaining that it wasn't fair because she was never allowed to visit a friend's house to play.

After everything had been quiet for a time the child appeared and tried again, this time using a different reason why her mother should relent and allow her to spend the afternoon with her friend: 'Mum, I've been in my room thinking about what you said, but Jesus told me I could go.'

The tired mother looked at her daughter and replied, 'Well, Jesus didn't tell me.'

The daughter looked into her mother's eyes and said, 'Mum, you weren't listening!' With that she gave up and began to play with her own toys.

Now the young girl had obviously made up her reasons for visiting her friend, but there are two great truths in the story that we should note. The first is that God does speak to us. The second is that we all should take notice of what he has said.

In the Garden of Eden God actually walked with Adam in the cool of the evening and spoke to him, using a voice that Adam could hear. If we go to the last book of the Bible we read that John was 'in the Spirit on the Lord's Day' (Revelation 1:10) and there in that state heard God speaking with a loud voice which sounded like a trumpet.

In the book of Daniel we find that God revealed his plans through dreams to Nebuchadnezzar. God then gave Daniel the interpretation of that dream 'in a night vision' (Daniel 2:19). Isaiah spoke of having a 'vision' (Isaiah 1:1). The Lord revealed his intentions to Joseph and Mary by means of an angel (Matthew 1:20).

The writer to the Hebrews says that in the 'last days' God spoke to us 'by his Son' (Hebrews 1:1-2). The disciples heard Jesus speaking to them. He taught them the truth, which they wrote totally free from any error.

Those who wrote the Scriptures were inspired men who wrote only truth because the words were given them by God. The New Testament as we have it today is the translation of God's final revelation to mankind. Nothing God wanted us to know has been left out, and there is nothing more to be revealed.

How then can I say that God still speaks to me? I can't hear an audible voice, but I do know what God is saying to me. How? By reading the Scriptures! God today speaks to us through his Word, through the sixty-six books that make up the Bible.

God speaks, but the real problem is that very few people bother to listen. There is a Bible in almost every house in the Western world, but most people don't bother to open it and read. Jesus told his disciples that the Holy Spirit would guide them into the truth: 'However, when he, the Spirit of truth, has come, he will guide you into all truth; for he will not speak on his own authority, but whatever he hears he will speak; and he will tell you things to come' (John 16:13).

The self-same Holy Spirit is the one who interprets his words for us. As we read our Bibles we should be praying that the Holy Spirit might guide us into all truth, remembering that 'All Scripture is given by inspiration of God, and is profitable for doctrine, for reproof, for correction, for instruction in righteousness, that the man of God may be complete, thoroughly equipped for every good work' (2 Timothy 3:16-17). May the Bible be your Book!

The law of the LORD is perfect, converting the soul;
The testimony of the LORD is sure, making wise the simple;
The statutes of the LORD are right, rejoicing the heart;
The commandment of the LORD is pure, enlightening the eyes;
The fear of the LORD is clean, enduring forever;
The judgements of the LORD are true and righteous altogether.
More to be desired are they than gold, yea, than much fine gold;
Sweeter also than honey and the honeycomb.
Moreover by them your servant is warned,
And in keeping them there is great reward

(Psalm 19:7-11).

To think about

1. Why is the Word of God so precious?
2. Why should Christians read their Bible?
3. In what way could we say that a Bible is like a mirror to each one of us?
4. How many books are there in the Old Testament and in the New Testament?
5. Name two books of the Bible you have read completely.

Pluck the peas?

> '...walk worthy of the Lord, fully pleasing him, being fruitful in every good work and increasing in the knowledge of God...' (Colossians 1:10).

Read
• • • • • • • • • • • • • • • • • •
Jeremiah 21:11-14

There are many places in the Scriptures where we read the word 'fruit'. Not only trees produce fruit; in God's Word we are told that people produce either good or bad fruit. This means we must look at our own life and determine what 'fruit' we are producing, because this will be an indication of our relationship with the Lord Jesus.

We have a house on a small plot of land, and the only fruit we have growing are a few grapes, lemons and grapefruit. When our family was

young and hungry, Val and I had a vegetable garden.

A friend who had grown up in a city was appointed to a one-teacher school in the country. He and his family had never lived in the country, but they looked forward to the change in lifestyle. He had never grown vegetables, but now that he was surrounded by farmers, it was suggested that he should commence a vegetable garden.

One humorous farmer gave him some climbing pea seeds and told him to plant them beside a fence and then wait for the crop. The seeds were planted and every day they waited and watched. The pea plants grew up the fence and one day as the farmer rode by on his horse he looked over the fence and said, 'Bill, you will have a good crop of peas by the look of all those flowers on the vines, but have you plucked them yet?'

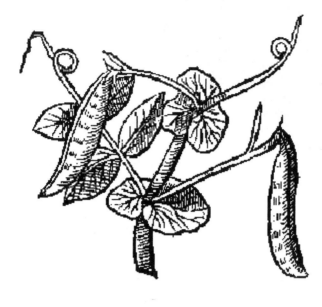

'What do you mean?' asked Bill.

'You have to "pluck" the yellow centre out of the flower to let the pea pods grow out,' the farmer ordered.

'I didn't know you had to do that,' Bill replied, 'but I'll do it today.'

Of course the farmer rode off with a big smile on his face. Bill plucked all his pea flowers and waited for his crop of peas. He ended up being the object of much laughter as he told people that he was expecting a big crop of fruit. However, nothing happened. When he discovered he had been tricked he dug out the peas and planted different vegetable seeds.

The Scriptures tell us that as Christians we must produce spiritual fruit that is worthy of our profession of faith in Christ. In our reading we find the nation of Judah being warned of her forthcoming judgement because of her evil ways. The Lord spoke very plainly when he said, 'But I will punish you according to the fruit of your doings' (v. 14). God's people had turned away from Jehovah to serve the gods of the surrounding nations. No longer were they fully obedient to the commands of God, who had chosen them as his own people. God's judgement was severe as Judah was taken into captivity by the Babylonians for seventy years. God expects the fruit of righteousness from his people!

John the Baptist warned the people of Israel, especially the spiritual rulers, that judgement was about to fall on the nation and urged them to 'bear fruits worthy of repentance' (Matthew 3:8).

When a sinner is born again the Holy Spirit begins the work of making that person holy. The repentant Christian begins to hate sin, which is the fruit of our sinful nature and the flesh. In place of that fruit we find the 'fruit of the Spirit' which is 'love, joy, peace, longsuffering, kindness, goodness, faithfulness, gentleness [and] self-control' (Galatians 5:22-23).

Our text commands us to be fruitful in good works that will bring praise and glory to Christ. Why not closely examine your own life and personality to see if you are exhibiting the 'fruit of the Spirit'?

The righteous shall flourish like a palm tree,
He shall grow like a cedar in Lebanon.
Those who are planted in the house of the LORD
Shall flourish in the courts of our God.
They shall still bear fruit in old age;
They shall be fresh and flourishing,
To declare that the LORD is upright;
He is my rock, and there is no unrighteousness in him

(Psalm 92:12-15).

To think about

1. What fruit do you have growing in your garden?
2. In the parable spoken by Christ in John 15:1-8, what is necessary to produce spiritual fruit?
3. What is the end of people who do not produce 'the fruit of the Spirit'?
4. If you are a Christian, why do you do good works? Read John 15:14 and Ephesians 2:10.

Climbing over the fence

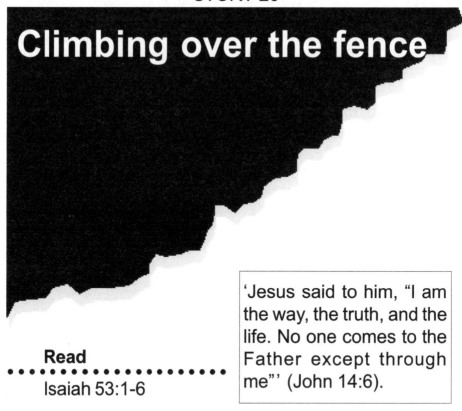

Read
• • • • • • • • • • • • • • • • • •
Isaiah 53:1-6

'Jesus said to him, "I am the way, the truth, and the life. No one comes to the Father except through me"' (John 14:6).

Most Western countries suffer from the problem of illegal immigrants and Australia is no different. As I write these words, the news is being broadcast of another boatload of illegal immigrants being detained. These people have risked their lives crossing oceans, sometimes in a boat that is very unseaworthy.

One boatload landed undetected on the northern coast of Australia where they faced the danger of crocodiles and having no food. Fortunately they were all found and taken to detention centres before being sent back to their homelands.

They had entered Australia the wrong way. Our country accepts many immigrants from all countries, but it means making an application to ensure

they are suitable people. Like other nations we don't want criminals entering the land. Migrants must have their

health checked out and at times there are re-
strictions placed upon applicants where there
is little opportunity for them to find work. Australia has a 'family reunion' programme where
settlers are able to bring to Australia other
members of their family. Our hope is that after
some time the migrants will become citizens of
their new country.

However, at the moment we find 'boat
people' making illegal entry into our nation.
Most are caught by our naval ships, but I'm
sure that many slip through our security
network.

Christ has a kingdom — the kingdom of God — and sinners are invited
to take up citizenship. However, all intending citizens must enter by the only
method, which is a saving faith in the Lord Jesus Christ. The Lord Jesus is
the doorway into God's kingdom and those who sneak in by some other
way cannot become citizens of the kingdom of heaven. Peter taught this
truth very plainly: 'Nor is there salvation in any other, for there is no other
name under heaven given among men by which we must be saved' (Acts
4:12).

John Bunyan knew this truth and had a man called Ignorance claim: 'I
know my Lord's will, and have been a good liver; I pay every man his own;

I pray, fast, pay tithes, and give alms, and have left my country, for whither
I am going.' Here was a man who believed that by doing things he could
save himself. He failed to understand that salvation was only possible through
faith in Christ. Keeping God's law does not save! Keeping the law is usually
one of the evidences of having entered the Way through Christ.

Formalist and Hypocrite had not entered by the wicket gate. They thought
they knew a short cut into the kingdom of God. They climbed over a wall
and claimed it didn't matter how they entered the Way to heaven — all that
mattered to them was that they believed they were on the Way. The way to
paradise is through Christ and by the cross, where sins are washed away.
Christian, then, do not follow other ways as they lead to hell.

Australia's illegal immigrants are sent home and told to fill out an application form in order that they might enter the correct way. Then they may be able to enter the country and enjoy the privileges of the land by gaining full citizenship.

Today's reading is of the saving work of Christ, who died to save sinners who had 'gone astray' (v. 6). Did God's 'Servant' die for you?

> Show me your ways, O LORD;
> Teach me your paths.
> Lead me in your truth and teach me,
> For you are the God of my salvation;
> On you I wait all the day
>
> (Psalm 25:4-5).

To think about

1. We talk about Christ saving his people — how did Christ save his people?
2. What does a Christian mean when he says he is 'saved'?
3. Where were Christ's people first called Christians? (The answer is found in Acts 11.)
4. In Isaiah 52:13 the 'Servant' of God is revealed. Who is this 'Servant' and why is he called a 'Servant'?

Be kind to pigs

Read
• • • • • • • • • • • • • • • • • • • •
Luke 6:27-36

'And just as you want men to do to you, you also do to them likewise' (Luke 6:31).

The mark of a Christian is love — love of God and love of our fellow man. This love is to be of all people, even our enemies. Of course, everyone finds it hard to 'love' the drunkard lying in the gutter, but the love that God speaks about is one that overcomes our feelings. Christians should be able to show their 'love' for the drunk in the street by helping him before he gets

hurt. It means going out of our way to help people who deserve nothing, because that is exactly what God did for his people — he reached down and saved sinners who rebelled against him. He 'loved' his people before time began and saved them both 'in' their sins and 'from' their sins.

Pig hunting is a popular sport amongst some people in Australia as wild pigs are considered vermin in many areas. These animals tear up the soil and help cause erosion, which has ruined great areas of the land. Hunters head off into the outback and return with stories of their exciting hunts.

One group of hunters had a rather humorous but distressing story to tell about their venture. They should have showed kindness to the pigs by killing them quickly and without too much suffering, but the men had a cruel plan. They parked their expensive four-wheel drive near some scrub where they knew pigs could be found. When they saw a small pig asleep they crept up and threw a net over it. They put a strap around the frightened pig, under which they placed a stick of dynamite. After lighting the fuse they let it escape. The plan was that the animal would run to where the other pigs were hiding and when the dynamite exploded they would be able to shoot the pigs that came running out of the bush.

The frightened pig ran for his life and for some reason, seeing the four-wheel drive, ran under it. The men immediately saw what was about to happen so began to yell out at the pig, who by that time had caught the strap on the exhaust system. The strap became loose, the dynamite fell to the ground and the frightened animal escaped safely into the bush.

The men could do nothing, as none were sure they could get the dynamite from under their vehicle before it exploded. They just watched as their very expensive car was suddenly blown apart. The man who told me the story said it was an amazing scene, especially as the fuel tank also exploded. The unkind act had resulted in a big financial loss!

You and I should show kindness to all of God's creatures, not just people. In today's reading Jesus tells us that we should pray for all people, especially those who hurt us. If someone in need asks for some warm clothing and we have some to spare we should give it to him without expecting anything in return. Even if someone hurts us we have no right to take personal revenge. To be filled with anger, resentment and desire for revenge is sin, and sin has no place in the life of any person, especially the Christian.

94

This teaching is hard for us to follow, but Christ has set us the example. When he was struck on the face (John 18:22-23) he didn't respond in anger by calling down the wrath of God on them.

We do have every right to use the law of the land to defend us from evil men and women and this is taught in the Scriptures: 'But if you do evil, be afraid; for he [the ruler] does not bear the sword in vain' (Romans 13:4). Our government is appointed by God and we must obey all lawful commands of our rulers. If the law of the land says stealing is wrong and someone steals some of our possessions, we allow the police to take action on our behalf to put things right. We have no right to take personal revenge by burning down the thief's house or stealing all his possessions. We are to show Christian love, which is a gentle kindness done only for the good of the other person and the glory of God. In other words, we do to others just what we'd like them to do to us. Is this your character? If you profess to be a Christian this should be your character.

Depart from evil, and do good;
And dwell for evermore.
For the LORD loves justice,
And does not forsake his saints

(Psalm 37:27-28).

To think about

1. What is Christian love? Read 1 Corinthians 13:4-8.
2. How can you show love to your schoolteacher?
3. What would you do if a school pupil smashed your bicycle?
4. How did Jesus show love?

It's dark outside!

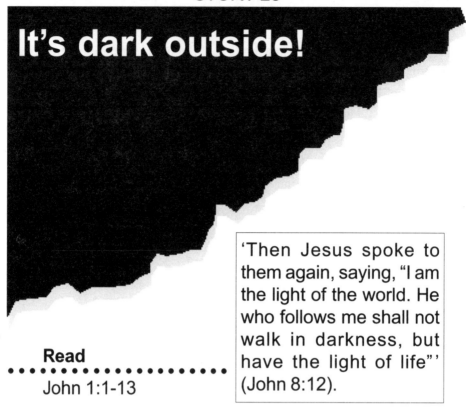

'Then Jesus spoke to them again, saying, "I am the light of the world. He who follows me shall not walk in darkness, but have the light of life"' (John 8:12).

Read
● ● ● ● ● ● ● ● ● ● ● ● ● ● ● ● ●
John 1:1-13

Many young children will not sleep in a darkened room and parents make an effort to provide a night light. Even adults at times find the darkness to be

frightening. Once I was in a cave, deep underground, when the lights were turned off. It was so dark I could feel the darkness and was pleased when the lights were turned back on.

Jesus said very plainly that he is the light of the world. In 1 John 1:5 we also read, 'This is the message which we have heard from him and declare to you, that God is light and in him is no darkness at all.' God is holy and pure light. There is no darkness or sin in our God. He cannot bear to look upon sin as it is so vile in his eyes: 'You are of purer eyes than to behold evil, and cannot look on wickedness' (Habakkuk 1:13).

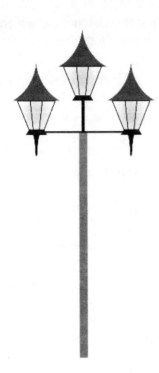

Jesus is 'the true Light' of the world (John 1:9) and all who follow him reflect his light. John the Baptist was a 'light bearer', as are all of God's people. It is as if Christ is the sun and Christians are moons, reflecting his light.

Night is the time when most criminals carry out their wicked works. We are very pleased that the local council has a street light in front of our house, which I'm sure is a deterrent to people with plans to break into our home.

In the Scriptures, that which is wicked and evil in God's eyes is described as 'darkness'. If you are a Christian, these words of the apostle Paul will have meaning, because Christ has delivered you 'from the power of darkness, and translated [you] into the kingdom of the Son of his love' (Colossians 1:13).

Some of my older readers will remember the days of the last war when the law required homes to be in darkness during the night. Enemy planes were searching for places to bomb and it was possible that lights would be the means of finding a target.

In Australia there was no probability of bombing in the area in which we lived, but the law still required darkness at night-time. My parents took out a tin of black paint and painted the windows to prevent any light escaping. During the night, wardens moved about checking to ensure no light could be seen. Silver iron roofs were painted to prevent them reflecting the moonlight. For safety, darkness was demanded from everyone at night because evil was on the prowl. For many years after the war our windows were still blackened and remained a continual reminder of the dangerous war days.

A pastor friend often took his pet dog for a walk after teatime. As it was dark he usually carried his cricket bat for protection. In our homes we have lights burning to prevent us walking into the furniture or the doorway. Light is needed for survival.

We don't like darkness, yet most people are members of the kingdom of darkness and do not realize it until it is too late. In the parable of the wedding feast where one guest was incorrectly dressed, we read that the servants were commanded by the king: 'Bind him hand and foot, take him away, and cast him into outer darkness; there will be weeping and gnashing of teeth' (Matthew 22:13).

When God created the universe, the first thing to be created out of the darkness was 'light' (Genesis 1:3). When this sinful world has run its course there will be new heavens and a new earth brought into existence, in which total righteousness is found. In that new creation we are told there will be no need of the sun or moon to provide light because '...the glory of God illuminated it. The Lamb is its light' (Revelation 21:23). Sin, or darkness, has no place in God's new eternal kingdom.

May each of my readers know they have a place in God's eternal kingdom of light.

Righteousness and justice are the foundation of your throne;
Mercy and truth go before your face.
Blessed are the people who know the joyful sound!
They walk, O LORD, in the light of your countenance

(Psalm 89:14-15).

To think about

1. What is meant by the expression, 'God is light'?
2. In Matthew 5:16, we are told to let our light shine in this world. What does this mean?
3. In Habakkuk 1:13 we read that God cannot bear to look upon wickedness. What does this mean?
4. Why do you think hell is described as 'outer darkness'?

It's dangerous fishing on the rocky headlands

Read
• • • • • • • • • • • • • • • • •
1 Corinthians 15:1-11

'And Thomas answered and said to him, "My Lord and my God!"' (John 20:28).

We are surrounded by death. Daily we read in our newspapers the long lists of names of people who have died and are to be buried. Had there been newspapers in the day of the Lord Jesus I'm sure there would have been a notice in the Gentile Sabbath paper, *The Jerusalem Daily*, of the crucifixion and death of the 'King of the Jews' and two criminals. Christ died that day and his death was witnessed by many people. It was a big news event.

Recently in a nearby large coastal city, a well-known fisherman disap-

peared while he was fishing from a rocky headland. The TV news showed the huge waves crashing onto the rocks and again there was the warning that fishermen should take extreme care when fishing from these dangerous spots. When the man's wife was interviewed she broke down and wept at the thought that her husband had been drowned. As the man's body had not been found, the water police indicated that

they would search the area, helped by a helicopter. Then the reporter said that all that had been found were some of the man's fishing gear and his car, which was parked nearby.

A week later it was again reported that the fisherman's body had not been found and a thought passed through my mind — maybe he doesn't want to be found. Perhaps he disappeared in order to start a new life somewhere else in Australia.

Three months later someone reported that the 'drowned' fisherman had been seen in a distant city, and then came the revelation that one of his bankcards had been used. The suspicions of the police grew and eventually it was announced that the 'dead' man had been arrested for being a 'public nuisance'. The dead man was alive! We read in the paper that he didn't want to return to his family. He had faked his death in order to get away from his wife and children and start life over again. He was a wicked man!

When the Lord Jesus was killed on the cross there was no doubt that he was dead. The rough, tough soldiers on duty that day had seen death before and knew that Christ was dead. As a result they didn't break his legs to hasten his death (John 19:33).

In order to prevent anyone stealing Christ's body from the tomb and then claiming he had risen from the grave, soldiers were placed on guard. When the angels arrived to witness the resurrection of the Lord and carry out their duties, those frightened soldiers ran away. Later they were bribed to lie and report that the disciples had stolen Jesus' body.

However, there followed a series of events, which, if they happened today, would be accepted as ample proof that a resurrection had indeed taken place.

The disciples and others saw an empty tomb. Outside the tomb Mary Magdalene saw and spoke with Christ. On the evening of the same day (Sunday) Christ appeared and spoke with the disciples who were

hiding from the authorities. He showed them his nail-pierced hands and feet, and his side where he had been wounded by a Roman spear.

A week later Christ again appeared and Thomas, who was absent that first Sunday, acknowledged him as his 'Lord' and his 'God' (John 20:28). Our reading goes on to give more proof that Christ was risen from the dead. He had appeared to over five hundred people on one occasion. And last of all he spoke to the apostle Paul on the road to Damascus (Acts 9:4-6). There was ample eyewitness evidence to the historical fact that Christ was no longer dead, but lived!

The eyewitnesses to the resurrection suffered cruelly as they went about preaching the resurrection. To suffer such terrible treatment shows they were either mad or really believed what they said. The resurrection of Christ was not some faked event. There was sufficient evidence to prove the claims of the writers of the Scriptures. However, today we have professing Christians, especially some church leaders, who deny the resurrection. These people have no right to claim to be Christians.

Do you believe that the Lord Jesus lived, died and rose again? Your salvation is bound up in the reply you give to that question. One day, just as Christ rose again, so will all people, some to glory and others to damnation. What will be your situation on that day when Christ returns?

I have set the LORD always before me;
Because he is at my right hand I shall not be moved.
Therefore my heart is glad, and my glory rejoices;
My flesh also will rest in hope.
For you will not leave my soul in Sheol,
Nor will you allow your Holy One to see corruption

(Psalm 16:8-10).

To think about

1. Who was the first disciple to enter the empty tomb?
2. By what nickname do people today know Thomas? What does it mean?
3. Christ rose from the dead in his resurrected body. Where is Christ today?
4. What happens to a Christian when he dies? See Philippians 1:21-23.

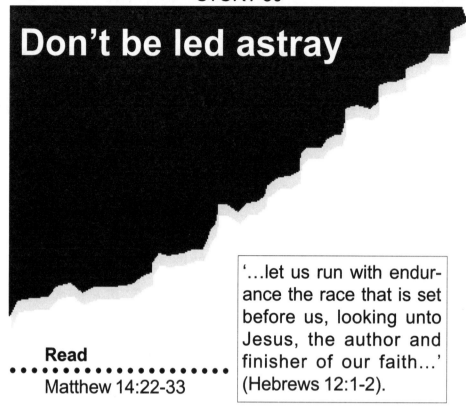

Don't be led astray

Read
....
Matthew 14:22-33

'...let us run with endurance the race that is set before us, looking unto Jesus, the author and finisher of our faith...' (Hebrews 12:1-2).

The chosen people of Israel knew the words of Isaiah 45:22: 'Look to me, and be saved, all you ends of the earth! For I am God, and there is no other.' Those who loved God looked to him for they knew that salvation was found in him alone.

Paul, the great apostle, has set an example of Christian living that the saints would do well to follow. Like any good soldier he was willing to suffer everything for the Lord Jesus he loved. He followed Christ, living a life of righteousness. Like the athlete at the Olympic Games who obeyed the strict rules for training and competing, he lived according to the rules of faith. His Christian life was run with his eyes firmly settled on Jesus Christ in whom he had found salvation.

Paul knew that to turn aside was to invite disaster for his spiritual life. He fully believed what he had written to the Corinthians: 'But I discipline my body and bring it into subjection, lest, when I have preached to others, I myself should become disqualified' (1 Corinthians 9:27). There was no turning aside for the apostle Paul.

One day Wags escaped from our yard just as the postman was delivering the mail. A motorbike was a new experience for him so he set off after it. The postman was unconcerned as the dog kept his distance. When the bike stopped so did Wags, making sure there was several metres between himself

and the postman. When Val saw what had happened, Wags was about fifty metres down the road, so she set off after him. The postman led the way, followed by Wags and then Val. When the postman stopped to deliver the mail, so did Wags. When the bike started off, so did Wags. As the distance between Val and Wags increased, Wags kept his eyes on the motorbike and Val kept her eyes on Wags.

Val was becoming exhausted. Our dog was about one hundred metres along the road and the distance between the two was increasing. Val was about to give up and return home to get the car when Wags suddenly stopped and looked towards a nearby house. Something had caught his attention and he was no longer looking at the motorbike. His eyes were centred on the large dog that was looking over the fence and barking. Slowly he moved towards the fence, only to be caught by Val and returned to his own garden.

Val said she'd never have been able to run him down as long as he was looking at the postman on his motorbike. As soon as he looked away he could be caught.

Wags' behaviour reminds me of a Christian who finds his spiritual life going along at a fine pace as long as he has his eyes upon his Lord Jesus. Satan tries to gain his attention with the pleasures of the world, the flesh and his own special delights. When the Christian looks away from Jesus, he easily falls into sin.

When Peter saw Jesus walking across the water, he stepped onto the sea and, with his eyes firmly fixed upon his Lord, walked out in faith. There was

Peter moving across the water towards Jesus, until he took his eyes off his Lord and saw the waves. Immediately he began to sink!

The saints find it much easier to walk in the steps of the Lord while we have our eyes fixed upon him. We read the Scriptures, pray, attend worship and mix with Christian friends. As soon as we begin to neglect these vital parts of our Christian life we find our relationship with Christ beginning to waver. Satan's snares are successful when we start living for ourselves and our own pleasure. Several times the fear of the Jews resulted in Peter falling into sin. He denied Christ just before the crucifixion (Matthew 26:30-35). Another occasion was at Antioch where the fear of the Jews resulted in him teaching that Gentiles had to be circumcised before they could become Christians (Galatians 2:11-21).

We are no different to Peter, and the fear of what our friends and neighbours might say because we follow Christ can cause us to hide our faith and begin to live like the worldling. We must keep our eyes firmly fixed upon Jesus and follow him till life's end. Then we will be able to say with the apostle Paul: 'I have fought the good fight, I have finished the race, I have kept the faith. Finally, there is laid up for me the crown of righteousness, which the Lord, the righteous Judge, will give me on that day' (2 Timothy 4:7-8). Can you say this?

> All the ends of the world
> Shall remember and turn to the LORD,
> And all the families of the nations
> Shall worship before you.
> For the kingdom is the LORD's,
> And he rules over the nations
>
> (Psalm 22:27-28).

To think about

1. Why is it important to keep our eyes upon the Lord Jesus Christ?
2. Jesus is in heaven today. How can we obey the command to keep our eyes upon him?
3. Paul looked forward to a 'crown of righteousness'. What does this mean?

What's the point to the story?

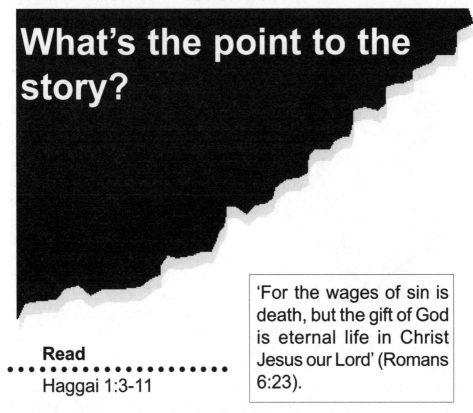

Read
· · · · · · · · · · · · · · · · · ·
Haggai 1:3-11

'For the wages of sin is death, but the gift of God is eternal life in Christ Jesus our Lord' (Romans 6:23).

All workers look forward to receiving their wages — a fair pay for a day's work. Families use their wages to meet the basic needs of life. Christian families should always put aside a portion to support the Lord's work. In our society, even those without work look forward to receiving some regular form of government support.

The Bible tells us that sin pays terrible wages — death! That means both physical death and spiritual death in eternal hell. Faith in Christ also pays wages, which are all of grace. Peter wrote that all saints were assured of 'an inheritance incorruptible and undefiled ... that does not fade away, reserved in heaven for you' (1 Peter 1:4). Our text tells us very plainly of the wages of both sin and saving faith.

A friend who had several horses found one to be a real pest. It kept getting through a fence and into the shed where the horse feed was stored. Each morning the owner found the horse enjoying himself as he gorged on the delicious hay. So the farmer put up a better fence; but the following day the horse had

successfully forced his way through the barrier once again and had enjoyed eating the forbidden food. The farmer tried once again, but the horse forced his way through the new fence once more. From that night onwards the horse was tethered in the paddock so he couldn't get to the feed shed.

A couple of days later the horse looked ill and wasn't interested in food, but the farmer thought he was sick because he had overeaten. As the days passed and the horse's condition worsened, a veterinary surgeon was called. He looked down the horse's throat, did everything that vets should do, and announced that the horse was seriously ill, although he wasn't sure what the problem was.

He gave the horse an injection and asked the farmer to contact him if its condition became worse. As he was leaving, he gave the horse a friendly pat on the stomach and as he did he let out a loud yell: 'Ouch, what was that!'

He looked at his hand to find blood oozing from a scratch. Then he looked at the horse's stomach and to his surprise found the sharp point of a bag-needle protruding from the horse's hide. A 'bag-needle' in Australia is a large, slightly curved needle that is used to sew up bags, using a strong string. Taking out a large pair of tweezers he pulled the long needle from the horse and pronounced him cured.

The horse had apparently swallowed the bag-needle when he had broken into the shed. Somehow the needle had found its way into the hay and it was no wonder the horse felt sick. The result of the horse doing what he should not have done was sickness and the possibility of death.

The apostle Paul wrote of the Corinthians who were getting drunk and overeating at the Lord's Supper. The Communion

service simply became a party. God chastened these people with sickness and, in some cases, death. So we see that sin pays wages, even for God's people.

Our reading today is about the Jews, who had returned from the captivity in Babylon, but failed to finish the building of God's temple. They had lost their spiritual way and instead of finishing the Lord's work had spent their time on their own homes. They had made sure their homes were fine constructions so they could live at ease, while the Lord's temple lay unfinished.

They did not understand that their sin had resulted in God causing poor seasons. They worked the soil and planted the crops, but the crops were not the best. They didn't have enough food on the table, or wine to drink. They were short of clothing and even their wages never seemed to be enough to meet all their needs. The people were being punished because they had put their own worldly living before the construction of God's temple where worship could be conducted, including the reintroduction of the sacrifices.

Sin pays wages even in this life — wages of disappointment, misery and unhappiness. Sin makes slaves of all her workers. Sin pays wages! Those who lived in Noah's time paid with their lives for their sinful living, but God saved faithful Noah and his family. On Judgement Day unrepentant sinners will be paid their wages — eternal death. All who love and serve the Lord Jesus will receive the gift of eternal life.

Maybe all of us need to make sure we are putting the things of God before what we want. Jesus told his hearers, who were concerned about material things such as money, clothing and other earthly possessions: 'Seek first the kingdom of God and his righteousness, and all these things shall be added to you' (Matthew 6:33).

If we have our priorities right, with God first, we shall be with Christ for ever. If not, eternal separation from God and all that is good will be our destiny.

Mark the blameless man, and observe the upright;
For the future of that man is peace.
But the transgressors shall be destroyed together;
The future of the wicked shall be cut off

(Psalm 37:37-38).

To think about

1. What should be the first priority in our life? Why do you say this?
2. What wages will all who serve Christ receive?
3. What wages do unrepentant sinners receive?
4. Who was Noah and what special promise did God give him? Read Genesis 9:11-17.

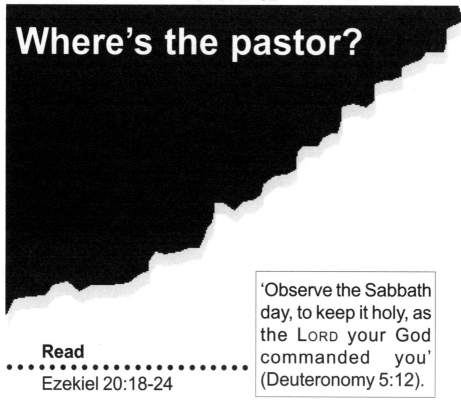

Where's the pastor?

Read
• • • • • • • • • • • • • • • • • • •
Ezekiel 20:18-24

'Observe the Sabbath day, to keep it holy, as the LORD your God commanded you' (Deuteronomy 5:12).

The nation of Israel had in their possession the Ten Commandments, which they were to obey. Our text is the commandment that required the people to keep holy one day in seven — the Sabbath. This was to be a day of rest for

Israel. The people were to rest their bodies in preparation for the coming six days of work and use the time to worship God. Failure to keep the Sabbath holy could result in serious punishment. We read in Exodus 31:15: 'Work shall be done for six days, but the seventh is the Sabbath of rest, holy to the LORD. Whoever does any work on the Sabbath day, he shall surely be put to death.'

Today Christians gather for worship on the first day of the week, the Lord's Day. Gone is the death penalty for breaking the Lord's Day, but Christians are to use this special day to the glory of God. The first day of the week was the day when the Lord Jesus rose from the dead. In those early days of the Christian church, the Jewish Sabbath was replaced by this new, special day.

Christians are to use the day for worship and kind deeds, but we must always remember that our time of worship is very important because during that time, together with our Christian friends, we glorify God, praise the name of the Lord Jesus and encourage one another to remain faithful.

A minister in a Sydney church was growing tired of the lax attitude to worship of some of his congregation. They were continually late for worship, yet he knew they were not late for their work obligations and other commitments. The worship of God was not a first priority in their lives and he decided to take dramatic action after appeals from the pulpit failed to bring about a change in habits.

One Sunday the minister was nowhere to be found at 11.00 a.m. The late arrivals walked in minutes late as usual and still the minister was missing. The elders held a discussion and some singing took place while everyone waited.

At 11.15 a.m. the minister walked in, up the aisle and into the pulpit. Then he preached an appropriate sermon concerning the obligations of Christian people to take the worship of God seriously. I understand his late arrival and challenging sermon solved the problem for some time in that congregation.

However, there are many people who still regularly arrive late for worship, which indicates the state of their heart. Some members of congregations spend their worship time checking the time and giving the impression they want to get their worship over and done with as quickly as they can. Some people can be seen checking to see if their watch is still working. This is nothing new as there were Jews who felt the same way about the worship of God. The Lord spoke to Israel through the prophet Amos about Jews who found the Sabbath an inconvenience. They were required to rest and worship all day, but in their minds they thought, 'When will the New Moon be past, that we may sell grain? And the Sabbath, that we may trade wheat?' (Amos 8:5).

Too many professing Christians have the idea that worship on the Lord's Day is just for one hour and they can't wait to get out of the church building and return to their pleasures.

Worship is a time of expressing our praise and love of Christ who died to save us from our sins. We should always spend some time before worship praying that God might bless both the minister and the congregation and we should always be on time. Christians should enjoy the time of worship, and then the Lord's Day becomes the best day of the week. We worship God 'in spirit and truth' (John 4:24), which means our mind is totally involved in worship and we carry out our worship in the only way possible, through the Mediator, the Lord Jesus Christ (1 Timothy 2:5).

After worship Christians have time to visit the sick and housebound, especially Christian people. The Christians of the early church used the day to collect money, which later would be used to help alleviate the distress of their Christian brothers and sisters in Jerusalem, who were suffering from food shortages. It is worth noting from Acts 11:29-30 and 1 Corinthians 16:2 that this was to be done on the first day of the week, implying that the Christians met on the first day of the week for worship!

There was a time when Christians had an early night on Saturday, in order to be wide awake for worship on the Lord's Day. Things have changed. Not many people today bother to bow their heads in prayer and spiritual meditation, in preparation for worship, when they take their seats.

The Jews were punished for treating the Sabbath Day with contempt. Their crops failed and their society fell into chaos. Finally, after many warnings, the people were taken into captivity by the Babylonians for seventy years.

May the worship of the Lord's Day be a delight to all of us, because it is a foretaste of heaven. May we always remember that the 'Lord's' Day is to be set aside for serving our God.

> I was glad when they said to me,
> 'Let us go into the house of the LORD.'
> Our feet have been standing
> Within your gates, O Jerusalem!

(Psalm 122:1-2).

To think about

1. What day of the week was the Jewish Sabbath?
2. Why were the Jews to rest on the Sabbath Day? (Read Deuteronomy 5:12-15.)
3. In what way can we make the Lord's Day a delight for both parents and children?

With a candle on my chest!

'But the natural man does not receive the things of the Spirit of God, for they are foolishness to him; nor can he know them, because they are spiritually discerned' (1 Corinthians 2:14).

Read
• • • • • • • • • • • • • • • • • •
2 Peter 1:16-21

In Story 24, I wrote, 'Jesus told his disciples that the Holy Spirit would guide them into the truth.' I explained that it was the Holy Spirit who guided the prophets, apostles and others in what they wrote to be included in the Bible. I explained that God still speaks to sinners through the Scriptures. But the question remains: 'How do we obtain the ability to understand what those godly men wrote?'

Our reading tells us plainly that all Scripture prophecy did not originate in the minds of the authors (v. 20. See the margin of your Bible for the alternative rendering of 'interpretation'.) God's words originated in the mind of God. It was the Holy Spirit who guided the writers of Scripture into all truth, and sinners need help to understand that God-given word.

In my study, I have hundreds of books. I once started to make a list of them all, but gave up after several days. If I need information I take down the appropriate book and start reading. However, before I can do that I must be able to read, and the room must be well lit.

When my wife was young her parents' farmhouse was not connected to electricity. Imagine the difficulties everyone faced. There was no electricity for the refrigerator, stove, washing machine, sewing machine and lights. Each night Val and her brother did their homework by the light of a lantern or a candle.

My father grew up on a farm where there was no electricity connected. Dad loved reading and often told me that he could not read in bed as his lamp or candle was on a table in the middle of the room. As there was no place to put the candle at the head of the bed for him to have the light falling on the page, he worked out a simple system to read the words. He put a small candle in the candleholder and placed it on one side of his chest. Then he could read the words as the glow from the candle flame fell on the page in his hands. He said that the biggest problem was the insects that fluttered around the light and kept flying into his eyes. He always had to be very careful not to fall asleep because the candle could easily fall onto the bedding and cause a fire. But with a light he could read.

I knew a pastor who could read his books in pitch darkness. He never turned on his lights at night-time when he was alone in the manse. Do you know why? He was blind! However, his books were illuminated by little raised dots — he could read Braille. Without those dots the words meant nothing!

To understand the meaning of God's Word we need illumination — spiritual illumination — illumination by the same Holy Spirit who inspired holy men to write. This is what is taught in our text.

Spiritual illumination, 'light', comes with the 'new birth' and without that miraculous work of God we would forever remain spiritually blind. The 'new birth' (John 3:5-6) brings saving faith in Christ, adoption into God's family, justification, sanctification and an understanding of spiritual truth. The writer to the Hebrews explained to the persecuted Christians that 'after [they] were illuminated, [they] endured a great struggle with sufferings'(10:32). After the 'new birth' they were given an unshakeable faith in Christ; a faith that would rather suffer death than deny their Saviour.

When you read your Bible and open the next page in your reading plan, you should pray sincerely that the Holy Spirit will guide you in understanding the truth of what you are reading. You should pray over the Word, meditate upon the Word and commit the Word to memory. Start this lifelong project while you are young and have an alert mind. But always remember that without the illumination of the Holy Spirit the Bible is just another book with many words written on many pages.

Teach me, O LORD, the way of your statutes,
And I shall keep it to the end.
Give me understanding, and I shall keep your law;
Indeed, I shall observe it with my whole heart

(Psalm 119:33-34).

To think about

1. What is Braille?
2. What illumination do sinners need before they can come to Christ for salvation?
3. What illumination do Christians need in order to understand the meaning of the Scriptures?
4. In our psalm portion the psalmist asks for 'understanding'. What does this mean?

A lovely Christian

Read
• • • • • • • • • • • • • • • • • • • •
Luke 13:20-30

'And indeed there are last who will be first, and there are first who will be last' (Luke 13:30).

If you handed a piece of paper and a pencil to a thousand people in the main street of a big city and asked them to write down the name of the person who was the finest Christian of this age, we would be very surprised at what we read. I think that the pope or Mother Theresa would be found written on most pieces of paper. Then would come some well-known archbishop whose

name continually appeared in the news. In the minds of most people it would be thought that these people held positions of greatest importance in the king-dom of God. The godly man or woman who faith-fully serves the Lord each day is forgotten and ignored. They are the nobodies of the world.

When the world thinks of 'great' people, it thinks of those whose names have been in the news as hav-ing done some great work or been presented with some medal or certificate. The world has it all wrong and the insignificant person who gives of his time and energy in a loving, quiet way is forgotten. Most of these lovely people will never be remembered in this world, except by a few whose lives were touched by them.

Have you ever been to a class reunion where the majority of old class-mates boast about their accomplishments and those who haven't become 'great' feel very much out of place? Many people want to be 'great' in the eyes of their friends and the world at large. Even two disciples, James and John, had a mother who wanted them to have positions of 'greatness' in Christ's kingdom: 'Grant that these two sons of mine may sit, one on your right hand and the other on your left, in your kingdom' (Matthew 20:21). This request greatly upset the rest of the disciples. Jesus reminded them: '…whoever desires to become great among you, let him be your servant' (Matthew 20:26).

I hadn't seen a school-mate for thirty-five years until when travelling by air a man with a beard approached me and asked, 'Are you Jim Cromarty?'

Soon we were talking about old times and old friends and within a few minutes we were speaking of our Christian experiences. We both loved the Lord Jesus. In our school days my friend was always at the bottom of the class. He found reading and spelling very difficult and school days were hard for him. But as we talked I discovered he was travelling to meet up with two 'prayer partners', which he did each year. They were two elderly ladies and he went down to their home to talk and pray, and to do any painting jobs and repair work their home needed.

He carried his Bible, the King James Version, with him, and together we read some favourite passages. He still mispronounced and stumbled over words. But he believed the church would soon face a difficult time when Christians would lose their Bibles. He had been committing his Bible to memory. He is the only person I know who can quote almost every psalm by heart, including Psalm 119. This friend, who years before couldn't spell and found reading difficult, could quote more Bible passages than I could.

His Mum and Dad later joined our congregation when they became too frail to travel to their Baptist church. My friend was a 'nobody' in this world, but in God's kingdom I felt that he was a great man. The love of Christ radiated from him and he was always out and about doing works of righteousness.

I thought of the text: 'And indeed there are last who will be first, and there are first who will be last.' Jesus knew that the Pharisees were the ones who expected to be first in the kingdom of God, not the Gentiles or the Jewish Christians. In fact that was what most Jews believed — the 'godly' Pharisees would be first in God's kingdom. But not so! The nobodies of the world who came to faith in Christ would be first in the kingdom of God. Christians who promoted themselves in the eyes of the world could well be last in Christ's kingdom. The faithful mother, who obeyed the commands of her Lord in caring for, praying for and teaching her children the things of the kingdom, could well be sitting very close to Christ at that royal, heavenly feast.

The nobodies of this world, who love Christ, are somebodies of importance in the eyes of God. The boastful Christian who loves the limelight will find that the humble, serving Christian is invited to a seat of importance, while he sits at the end of the table.

How true are the words of the apostle Paul: 'For you see your calling, brethren, that not many wise according to the flesh, not many mighty, not many noble, are called. But God has chosen the foolish things of the world to put to shame the wise, and God has chosen the weak things of the world to put to shame the things which are mighty; and the base things of the world and the things which are despised God has chosen, and the things which are not, to bring to nothing the things that are, that no flesh should glory in his presence' (1 Corinthians 1:26-29).

On Judgement Day there will be many surprises.

But I am poor and needy;
Make haste to me, O God!
You are my help and my deliverer;
O LORD, do not delay

(Psalm 70:5).

To think about

1. What can Christians do to please their Lord?
2. Who do you think will occupy positions of importance in Christ's kingdom? Why do you say this?
3. Often it is the 'nobodies' of the world that Christ saves. Why is this so?
4. What is Christ looking for in the character of his people?
5. What will be the surprises we hear and see on Judgement Day?

Followers

Read
• • • • • • • • • • • • • • • • • •
Mark 5:1-20

'Entreat me not to leave you, or to turn back from following after you; for wherever you go, I will go; and wherever you lodge, I will lodge; your people shall be my people, and your God, my God. Where you die, I will die, and there will I be buried. The LORD do so to me, and more also, if anything but death parts you and me' (Ruth 1:16-17).

Christianity is full of stories of people who, when they were converted, wanted to leave behind all that they once held dear, in order to follow Christ. If you are a Christian the same should be said of you.

John Paton had spent many years in the New Hebrides before he began to see men and women converted. One of his first conversions was Chief Namakei who had seen water filling the well that John had dug. No one believed that drinking water could be made to ooze up through the ground, as the natives had only seen fresh water fall from the clouds. A permanent water supply would be a great blessing to the natives, but they were all convinced that John Paton, 'Missi', was mad in what he was doing.

At last the well began to fill with water, but only after John had prayed for God to produce the precious liquid. When this happened Namakei knew in his heart that John's God was all John claimed him to be. On the Lord's Day after the well had filled, the chief addressed his people, 'We have laughed

117

at other things that Missi told us, because we could not see them. But from this day I believe that all he tells us about his Jehovah God is true. Some day our eyes will see it. For today we have seen rain from the earth … From this day, my people, I must worship the God who has opened for us the well, and fills us with rain from below. The gods of Aniwa cannot hear, cannot help us, like the God of Missi. Henceforth I am a follower of Jehovah God.'

Years later, faithful Namakei was dying and as he held John Paton's hand he said, 'O my Missi, my dear Missi, I go before you, but I will meet you again in the home of Jesus. Farewell.' And so the old Christian chief died. He was a converted cannibal, who became a devoted follower of Christ.

Think of that demon-possessed man you read about in today's reading. The whole countryside feared his madness. Often many strong men had tied him up, but he broke loose. Can you imagine how those men must have run for their lives as he chased after them? The demons so controlled him that they forced him to run about naked and he often cut himself. Those who lived near the tombs must have spent many sleepless nights as the poor fellow roamed about, crying out at the top of his voice.

The arrival of Jesus solved his problem. The demons were cast out and that once mad man now loved his Saviour. He wanted to follow Jesus wherever he went, but Jesus told him to go to his home and there bear witness to the great miracle the Lord had done for him. We are also to bear witness to our friends and relatives to the great work of salvation Jesus has accomplished for us. We are to live for Christ in our town and suburb. Everyone should know that we are his disciples.

Another lovely story about faithfulness to God is found in the book of Ruth. Naomi had spent many years in Moab where her husband and two sons died. She decided to return to her own people in the land of Israel, but she had two daughters-in-law who loved her. One girl, Orpah, said farewell to Naomi and said she would stay in the land of her birth. However Ruth thought differently. She loved her mother-in-law, but that was not all. She had been taught about Jehovah, the God of his people Israel. As Naomi was about to leave she urged Ruth to stay behind with her friends also, but Ruth had other ideas. Her words to Naomi are loved by godly people from all ages, throughout the world.

'Entreat me not to leave you,
Or to turn back from following after you;
For wherever you go, I will go;
And wherever you lodge, I will lodge;
Your people shall be my people,
And your God, my God.
Where you die, I will die,
And there will I be buried.

The LORD do so to me, and more also,
If anything but death parts you and me'

(Ruth 1:16-17).

How Ruth loved, not only Naomi, but also her God, Jehovah. Now she would follow Naomi back to the land of her people and her God. And that is the love that we should have for the Lord Jesus Christ, who gave himself that all of his people might have everlasting life.

May the God of Ruth and Naomi, the God of that demon-possessed man and the God of old Chief Namakei so captivate your heart and mind that you also leave everything to follow his Son, the Lord Jesus. As a disciple of Christ, you have eternal life. There is no other way in which to be saved.

When I remember you on my bed,
I meditate on you in the night watches.
Because you have been my help,
Therefore in the shadow of your wings I will rejoice.
My soul follows close behind you;
Your right hand upholds me

(Psalm 63:6-8).

To think about

1. Why do you think the healed demon-possessed man wanted to follow the Lord Jesus?
2. Why would any person want to follow Jesus?
3. What does Christ promise to all who follow him? (Read Luke 18:28-30.)
4. Was it Ruth or Naomi who was an ancestor of the Lord Jesus?

Oh, for a comfortable lap!

'...and the peace of God, which surpasses all understanding, will guard your hearts and minds through Christ Jesus' (Philippians 4:7).

Read
. . . .
Isaiah 26:1-6

There are times in our lives when all we want is peace and security. The affairs of the world begin to overwhelm us and we fear what will happen. Yet as Christians we have a God who has promised to give peace to his people. Why is it that we fear the opposition of the world and the assaults of Satan when really all we should fear is the Lord our God? Our God is all powerful and will certainly accomplish all of his purposes. He will not lose one of his people, no, not even the weakest saint. Christ has hold of the person with 'little faith' and will never let him go, no matter what fears fill his heart.

I didn't intend writing much about my dog Wags in this book, but a couple of months ago I saw something that amused me very much. A storm was brewing and in the distance we could see the jagged lightning flash followed by the sound of thunder. Wags, who, like most dogs, has very acute hearing, heard the thunder before we did and he came inside and began keeping very close to Val. When the thunder became louder he stood on his back legs and with two paws on her knees gave her the look of, 'Please pick me up. I'm frightened.'

Wags was once again very fearful. He'd heard thunder before and hated it. Soon he was sitting on Val's lap and trembling with fear. Val held him

close and patted him, and gradually the trembling lessened. He found peace of heart sitting on her lap.

Then in came the cat we were 'cat-sitting'. While the cat and dog tolerate each other, Wags nips her when he gets the chance and the cat is very watchful of Wags. We could see the cat was also frightened by the thunderclaps and needed some comfort. She came near to Val and then jumped up on the settee. Wags was still trembling, but as the cat came nearer he watched closely. The cat couldn't stand the thunder any more and made her move. She started to squeeze herself between Wags and Val, and finally there was Val with both the cat and dog, secure in her arms, both trembling with fear. There they remained till the thunder died away. While they were with Val they tolerated each other and the visible trembling disappeared. They found peace of heart being comforted on her lap.

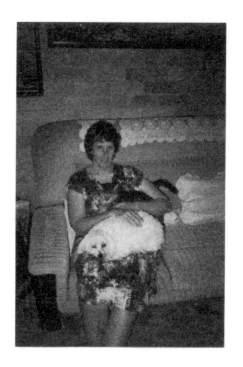

There are times in our lives when our hearts are fearful because of the events of the world about us or from Satan and his cruel temptations. I knew a dear Christian lady who was dying. Satan put it into her heart that all her sins were not forgiven and that she was dying unsaved. One of my elders spent much time with her in hospital, reminding her that all of her sins had been washed away by the precious blood of Christ. As she again looked to 'the God of peace' (Philippians 4:9), the 'peace of God' (Philippians 4:7) filled her heart and she died in the certain knowledge that she was safe with Jesus.

When our hearts are fearful, and the concerns of the world begin to drag us down, we must look to the God and Father of the Lord Jesus for the peace we need. Speaking through Isaiah, God comforted his troubled people of Judah: 'Say to those who are fearful-hearted, "Be strong, do not fear! Behold, your God will come with vengeance … he will come and save you"' (Isaiah 35:4). He is our comfort and Jesus invites us to come to himself for that promised peace. The disciples saw the power of Christ when the boat in which they were sailing was in danger of being swamped. 'Lord, save us! We are perishing!' they cried out (Matthew 8:25). Jesus awoke and stilled the storm and all was well. Their hearts were filled with peace and awe. They looked at the Lord Jesus in wonder while finding peace of heart in him.

Today's reading is God's promise of protection and peace for Judah, his covenant people. As his people trusted themselves to him their hearts would be filled with peace. Even Nebuchadnezzar, the mighty ruler they feared, would be brought low with a period of madness.

Today the same promise applies to the church. The gates of hell cannot destroy the church for whom Christ died and the saints' peace is to be found in him, because he is the 'Prince of Peace' (Isaiah 9:6).

May God grant us all that peace which is beyond the understanding of the world. May our hearts be always centred upon God and praise him for the salvation that is ours in Christ. A mind and heart fixed upon God is the only way to find that perfect peace.

You have put gladness in my heart,
More than in the season that their grain and wine increased.
I will both lie down in peace, and sleep;
For you alone, O LORD, make me dwell in safety

(Psalm 4:7-8).

To think about

1. What is fear?
2. What is meant by 'peace of heart'?
3. What do you fear in this world? How can you overcome that fear?
4. How can we obtain peace of heart from God?

The yoke is too heavy for me to carry

Read
••••••••••••••••
1 Kings 12:1-15

'Come to me, all you who labour and are heavy laden, and I will give you rest. Take my yoke upon you and learn from me, for I am gentle and lowly in heart, and you will find rest for your souls. For my yoke is easy and my burden is light' (Matthew 11:28-30).

King Solomon was dead and it was time for a new king to reign over God's people. The one to inherit his crown was his son Rehoboam who was soon to be crowned in Shechem. But the land would not belong to Solomon's son, because his father had broken God's laws and the kingdom would be torn away from him and given to his servant (1 Kings 11:9-13). The one who would become king of the ten tribes would be Jeroboam and this was announced to him by the prophet Ahijah (1 Kings 11:29-39).

When Rehoboam arrived at Shechem the people asked him to lighten the burden of taxes that his father Solomon had placed upon them. His aged, wise advisors also suggested he should do so, but Rehoboam was a fool and accepted the advice of his young, irresponsible comrades. His reply to his people was: 'My little finger shall be thicker than my father's waist! And now, whereas my father put a heavy yoke on you, I will add to your yoke; my father chastised you with whips, but I will chastise you with scourges!' (1 Kings 12:10-11). The yoke was the way in which animals carried their burdens. It was placed upon their shoulders so the animal could lift and pull.

In Australia, in days gone by, the timber workers used bullocks, yoked together, to drag logs out of the bush. In fact there are still some bullock teams being used in places where timber trucks cannot go. When a new, frisky bullock was to be  trained he would be yoked together with a quiet, good worker and for a week he would learn how to pull and work as a member of the bullock team. When he did all the pulling he soon found out that he carried the burden alone. When he slackened off he found the bullock driver's whip flicking his rump. He also found that the yoke with which he was linked to the good worker became most uncomfortable. He soon learned that working together lightened his load and life became easy.

The Pharisees of Christ's time placed heavy burdens upon God's people. They taught that salvation was only possible through obedience both to  God's law, and to all the extra laws they made. Spiritual life was a heavy burden for the people to carry and the Pharisees did nothing to lighten the load. Jesus was very critical of them: 'For they bind heavy burdens, hard to bear, and lay them on men's shoulders; but they themselves will not move them with one of their fingers' (Matthew 23:4).

Jesus invited those Jews who knew they were sinners, and were trying to earn salvation by their own works, to come to him and he would lighten their load. Like the young bullock which had to learn from the older bullock, Christ invited sinners, burdened by their heavy load of sin, to be yoked

125

to him and learn from him the way of salvation. Then they would find the way and burden light because he was the way of salvation and that salvation was not by works, but by faith. Christ's yoke is one of gentleness and humility, so unlike that of the Pharisees.

Spiritual rest is to be found only in Christ. Are you united to Christ by a God-given faith or are you still struggling with the burden of your sins and your own efforts to earn God's forgiveness?

> For my iniquities have gone over my head;
> Like a heavy burden they are too heavy for me...
> Do not forsake me, O LORD;
> O my God, be not far from me!
> Make haste to help me,
> O Lord, my salvation!

(Psalm 38:4, 21-22).

To think about

1. In what way can sins be a burden upon a person?
2. What is meant by 'faith in Christ'?
3. Name the first three kings of Israel.
4. Why was the kingdom of Israel torn in two?
5. Name the tribes that remained loyal to King Rehoboam.

The greatest wonder of all

> 'And I also say to you that you are Peter, and on this rock I will build my church, and the gates of Hades shall not prevail against it' (Matthew 16:18).

Read
• • • • • • • • • • • • • • • • • • •
Hebrews 12:25-29

I would like to test your knowledge by asking a question: Can you name the seven wonders of the ancient world? We hear them discussed, but few people know them all. Most people remember the 'Hanging Gardens of Babylon' and the Pyramids, but after that their memory fails them. The five usually forgotten are the 'Tomb of Mausolos'; the huge statue of Apollo known as

 the 'Colossus of Rhodes'; the 'Temple of Artemis', which was found at Ephesus; the statue of Zeus built at Rhodes; and in Alexandria there was King Ptolemy's great lighthouse.

They were built to last and were looked upon as great products of human ingenuity. But the majority are not to be found today. Which of the seven wonders of the ancient world are still with us in these days? If you search in your encyclopaedia you are sure to find a lot of information about these great monuments. You might like to make a list of what you consider to be

wonders of the modern world. I think the Taj Mahal and maybe the Sydney Opera House would make our list, but I know that within a few thousand years these beautiful buildings won't exist. The builders took great care constructing them, but time, wind, rain, earthquakes, war, pollution and so many other activities will eventually cause them all to fall apart. Nothing made by man really lasts.

The great Napoleon, when asked why he believed the teachings of the Bible, pointed to the Jewish people as his proof. He saw the continued existence of God's ancient, covenant people as a proof that what the Bible taught was truth. However, one day even the covenant race of Israel will be no more. The world on which we stand, which seems to us to be fixed and firm, will one day cease to exist. We are taught that when Christ returns everything as we know it will be changed: '…the heavens will pass away with a great noise, and the elements will melt with fervent heat; both the earth and the works that are in it will be burned up' (2 Peter 3:10). On that day the modern wonders of the world will be no more.

Our God does not change or age. As the words of Psalm 102 at the conclusion of this chapter remind us, other things will change, but not God. We can open our history books and find out that great nations rose to power and importance, but now cannot be found. Today the greatest power on earth is the USA, but in a century this might not be so. Rulers come and go, as do nations — nothing remains the same. Even you will change. I can look in the mirror and then at a photograph and see the differences.

However, there is a kingdom that cannot be destroyed by any power on earth — the kingdom of God, whose King is the Lord Jesus Christ. This kingdom has three sections: those who are now in paradise with Christ; those who serve Christ on this earth; and those who are yet to be born and who will be saved. These three groups make up the church of God. Every saint is a stone in the building and not one will be lost. In fact each one will be perfected on that day when the resurrection takes place and we have our perfect, sinless, glorified bodies.

On earth the church may appear battered and bruised, but it endures. Sometimes the church on earth may seem small, but it is probably much larger than we imagine. Elijah thought he was the last of God's people, but was told that some seven thousand had not bowed their knee to the false god, Baal (1 Kings 19:18).

When Christ returns there will be saints waiting to welcome him. Then the church will be presented to him as a beautiful bride (Ephesians 5:27) clothed in the righteousness of her Lord. Our reading speaks of a great shaking of the earth which will destroy everything, except the Lord's kingdom which remains, unshaken. The church of God will last for ever!

Are you part of that church, each member of which is saved by the precious work of Christ?

Of old you laid the foundation of the earth,
And the heavens are the work of your hands.
They will perish, but you will endure;
Yes, they will all grow old like a garment;
Like a cloak you will change them,
And they will be changed.
But you are the same,
And your years will have no end

(Psalm 102:25-27).

To think about

1. What part of you will last for ever?
2. Find out something about one of the wonders of the ancient world.
3. What does today's text teach us?
4. God does not change. How should this encourage Christians?

The great 'Peacemaker'

Read
• • • • • • • • • • • • • • • • • •
Ephesians 2:11-22

'But now in Christ Jesus you who once were far off have been brought near by the blood of Christ' (Ephesians 2:13).

The word 'peace' is a beautiful word. It sounds peaceful when you say it correctly and it speaks of a state of living that is best of all. Peace in my Collins dictionary is defined as 'the state existing during the absence of war'. There follows other definitions such as 'a state of harmony between people or groups'. I looked up the word 'peacemaker', which was defined as 'a person who establishes peace, especially between others'.

As I read my Bible I find the word 'peace' many times, so I decided to count the number of times it is found in my New King James Version of the Scriptures. Within seconds my computer told me that the word 'peace' was written 397 times!

We should all like peace, and those of my readers who are Christians know that God is at peace with all of his people, because we read: 'But he [Christ] was wounded for our transgressions, he was bruised for our iniquities; the chastisement for our peace was upon him, and by his stripes we are healed' (Isaiah 53:5). In other words, Jesus is our 'Peacemaker', yet he has

no such mention in the dictionary.

When I looked in the dictionary I expected to find another 'peacemaker' mentioned and was disappointed to find no mention of something that is of special interest to all who like 'Western' movies. When I was young we used to play cowboys and Indians. We had our home-made bows and arrows and our cap guns strapped to our waist. We'd practise 'drawing' our revolvers to see who was the quickest on the draw. It was good fun.

We used to call our revolvers 'Peacemakers'. In the 'old American West' the 'Peacemaker 45' was used in many situations to establish peace. They simply shot the opposition if they were quick enough and then an uneasy peace followed.

Following the resurrection of the Lord Jesus the disciples had good news to preach to the Jews and the Gentiles. Soon the church was growing, but there was trouble because the Jews disliked the Gentiles and didn't want them in the church. In the book of Galatians the Jews agreed to have the Gentiles as church members if they first of all became Jews; that is, they had to be circumcised.

In today's reading Paul reminded the Gentiles what they once were — they had no part in the kingdom of God, but were strangers to God and all his promises. However, Christ had come and died to save his people, both Jew and Gentile, and they were one! It was as if the big wall that once separated the two racial groups had been destroyed by Christ and now the two groups were united. The 'Peacemaker' was the Lord Jesus who in reconciling them to God made them brothers and sisters. They were all equal members in the church of God, all saved by the one Lord, sharing a common faith in Christ, born again by the same Holy Spirit and all on their way to the one destiny — paradise.

The 'Peacemaker' didn't act like the Colt revolver and destroy one group to bring about peace. Christ gave his own life to establish peace. Jesus is called the 'Prince of Peace' (Isaiah 9:6). The apostle Paul wrote that in the church, 'There is neither Jew nor Greek, there is neither slave nor free, there is neither male nor female; for you are all one in Christ Jesus' (Galatians 3:28).

The Lord Jesus Christ is the true 'Peacemaker' between God and man and between all racial groups. Has Christ made peace for you?

> The LORD sat enthroned at the Flood,
> And the LORD sits as King forever.
> The LORD will give strength to his people;
> The LORD will bless his people with peace

(Psalm 29:10-11).

To think about

1. Why were the American Red Indians called 'Indians'?
2. How did Christ make peace between the Jew and the Gentile Christians?
3. How did Christ make peace between God and his people?
4. Read Isaiah 9:6 and discuss what it says about the Lord Jesus.
5. What is the Jewish word for 'peace'?

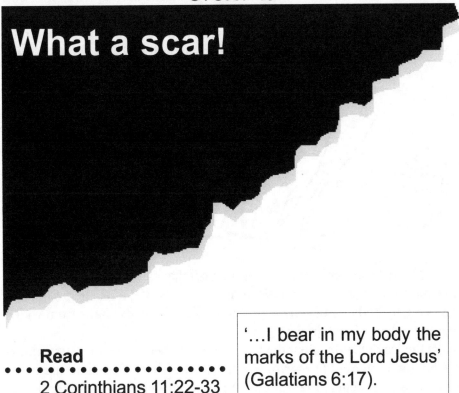

What a scar!

Read
· · · · · · · · · · · · · · · · · · ·
2 Corinthians 11:22-33

'...I bear in my body the marks of the Lord Jesus' (Galatians 6:17).

The apostle Paul travelled the known world preaching a risen Lord. Many people hated this 'good news' and they did all they could to have Paul stopped. Today's reading is a description of Paul's suffering for the Lord Jesus. I'm sure that all the apostles carried some scars that were the result of preaching the gospel.

If you look at your own body I'm sure most of you will find a scar or two which reminds you of something that happened to you. I have a long scar, about eight inches, on my right arm and I can still remember very clearly the time I had my fall.

Val's parents owned a farm and after one very big flood several acres of plants that were used to produce illegal drugs suddenly appeared. The Department of Agriculture said they would soon be out to poison the crop, but like many government departments it was some weeks before they came

to do the spraying. When I heard about the unusual plants we drove home to have a look. Val wasn't really interested, so I drove down to the paddock beside the river and made the decision to climb the barbed wire fence and collect some specimen leaves. To save undoing the gate I climbed to the top of the post and slipped. Down I fell into the wire. My trousers were almost torn off and then I saw blood everywhere. My arm had a severe gash with

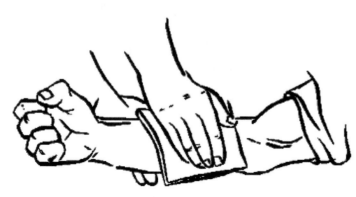 blood running everywhere. I looked at my leg and there saw cuts and gashes and more blood flowing.

I dragged myself carefully out of the barbed wire and drove home where it was decided that I should visit the doctor. He patched me up, gave me an injection and sent me home to rest. Now I have the permanent marks on my body, of the day I went to look at a field of plants from which people produce illegal drugs.

On the Day of Judgement the books will be opened and our faithfulness to Christ will be used to reward us. In a world where Christians are hated we will all carry scars of faithfulness in our body, whether in the flesh or in the mind. In our part of the world many Christians suffer the wounding, cruel words of ungodly people. Other Christians carry the marks of their faithfulness in their flesh.

The writer to the Hebrews wrote: 'Others were tortured, not accepting deliverance, that they might obtain a better resurrection. Still others had trial of mockings and scourgings, yes, and of chains and imprisonment. They were stoned, they were sawn in two, were tempted, were slain with the sword. They wandered about in sheepskins and goatskins, being destitute, afflicted, tormented — of whom the world was not worthy. They wandered in deserts and mountains, in dens and caves of the earth' (11:35-38).

Christ warned the disciples that they would be hated, just as he was despised: 'If the world hates you, you know that it hated me before it hated you. If you were of the world, the world would love its own. Yet because you are not of the world, but I chose you out of the world, therefore the world hates you' (John 15:18-19).

The Lord Jesus had the marks of his sacrificial death in his body. He was able to show the marks in his hands, feet and side to doubting Thomas, to prove he was the resurrected Lord Jesus. The apostle Paul likewise could point to the marks in his body that resulted from his faithfulness to the Lord Jesus.

The Christian life can be difficult, especially if we take seriously the command of the Lord to deny ourselves, take up our God-given cross daily, and follow the Lord Jesus (Luke 9:23). If you would like to read about the suffering of many godly people find a copy of *Foxe's Christian Martyrs of the World* and take notice of the faithfulness of Christ's people.

And when the difficult days come, remember that you must walk in the footsteps of your Lord and Master and consider it a privilege.

> The LORD builds up Jerusalem;
> He gathers together the outcasts of Israel.
> He heals the brokenhearted
> And binds up their wounds
>
> (Psalm 147:2-3).

To think about

1. Do you have any scars? Explain how you received your wound.
2. What scars does Christ carry in his body?
3. Can you think of (or name) any Christian who carries the scars because of his faithfulness to Christ?

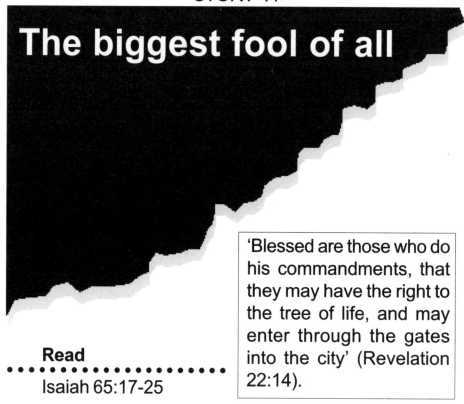

The biggest fool of all

'Blessed are those who do his commandments, that they may have the right to the tree of life, and may enter through the gates into the city' (Revelation 22:14).

Read
• • • • • • • • • • • • • • • • • •
Isaiah 65:17-25

Good things are in store for God's people! The life we now live should be lived in preparation for that day when we die and pass into the presence of Christ, or when the Lord returns the second time. This life is a preparation for that which is to come.

When Val and I go on holidays we find it a pleasant time making preparations for what we expect to enjoy. Before we left to go overseas we hired videos about Malaysia and Penang because we were going to spend a month visiting the country. We made sure we had foreign money to spend, hotel rooms were booked and some day trips were arranged. We found out all we could about the weather so we could wear appropriate clothes. We prepared for our journey. We were not like that foolish man in Christ's parable who made no preparations for his death (Luke 12:20). He prepared for retirement, but gave no thought to his unavoidable meeting with God.

Some time ago I read a story about such a fool. It went like this: A very rich nobleman had a jester who kept him smiling with his pranks and jokes. He enjoyed his jester and gave him a valuable ring with the order: 'You are to wear this ring until you meet someone who is a greater fool than yourself!'

The day came when the nobleman fell seriously ill and it was obvious he was dying. He called for his jester and said, 'Soon I will be leaving you.'

'Where are you going?' asked the jester.

'I'm going to another world,' replied the nobleman.

'When will you return?' asked the jester.

'Never,' came the reply.

'And what preparations have you made for your journey?' asked the concerned jester.

'None,' his master replied.

'What! None at all?' said the jester. Then he took the ring from his finger and as he handed it to his lord said, 'Here, take your ring.' The nobleman had made no preparations for his death. Have you?

At the moment of our death we will pass into eternity to face Christ, the Judge. There our eternal destiny will be made known. This is a journey every person must make. There can be no escape no matter who we are, or what power we have on earth. The Bible explains that we will each spend an eternity, with Christ in paradise, or in hell where we will suffer the punishment of God because of our sins. This is the 'lake of fire' (Revelation 20:15). Wise people, who know this truth, will prepare

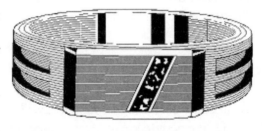

for that day just as sensible people prepare for their annual holidays.

I'm sure there are many people who, when they know the truth about heaven, say, 'I don't want anything to do with such a place!' The reason for such an attitude is that they love their sins and their sinful way of life. They want nothing to do with righteousness and serving the living God.

Others love God, Father, Son and Holy Spirit, and long to see the face of their Saviour. They want to be in the place of which the apostle John wrote: 'And I heard a loud voice from heaven saying, "Behold, the tabernacle of God is with men, and he will dwell with them, and they shall be his people. God himself will be with them and be their God. And God will wipe away every tear from their eyes; there shall be no more death, nor sorrow, nor crying. There shall be no more pain, for the former things have passed away." Then he who sat on the throne said, "Behold, I make all things new"' (Revelation 21:3-5).

All people like the idea of being where there is no more pain and no more death, but this is only possible where there is no more sin. The wages paid by sin is pain, sorrow and death. The Scriptures paint differing pictures of paradise, all of which should comfort the believer. In the letter to the church at Ephesus we read: 'To him who overcomes I will give to eat from the tree of life, which is in the midst of the Paradise of God' (Revelation 2:7). Here is the picture of the wonderful Garden of Eden before sin entered the world and ruined its beauty.

We are all on our way to a common destiny — the judgement seat of God. What follows we know in part, because of what God has revealed. We all must make that journey! The journey to hell requires that you do nothing, but continue to live in your sinful ways. The journey to paradise requires that you have a ticket that is freely available from God — saving faith in the Lord Jesus Christ.

In the midst of all the activities of life, remember to obtain that ticket to heaven. In other words, make preparations for the journey that you one day must make.

> The fool has said in his heart,
> 'There is no God.'
> They are corrupt,
> They have done abominable works,
> There is none who does good

(Psalm 14:1).

To think about

1. What is the best thing about paradise?
2. Name five people you expect to meet in heaven.
3. What is a 'jester'?
4. Why are people admitted to heaven?
5. What 'ticket' is needed to gain admittance to heaven?
6. Where do you get that ticket?

Sure, I'm a Christian!

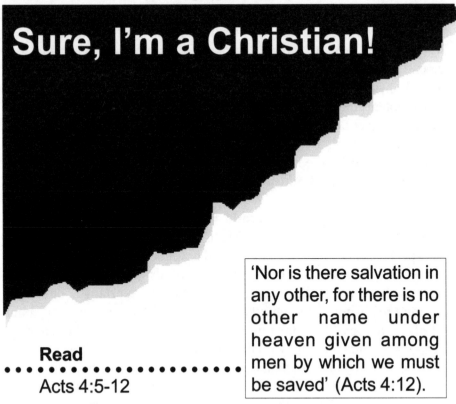

Read
• • • • • • • • • • • • • • • • • •
Acts 4:5-12

> 'Nor is there salvation in any other, for there is no other name under heaven given among men by which we must be saved' (Acts 4:12).

I once read in a book a searching question: 'If you were charged with being a Christian would there be enough evidence to convict you?' I started to seriously think about the question and decided that there was not that much evidence to prove to the neighbours that I was a Christian. We live in a country where no one is greatly concerned whether a person is a Christian or not. Most Christians have an easy life and their attitude generally is, 'All is comfortable. Why rock the boat?'

I have been interested in several court cases. One was concerning 'the headless body' where a body was discovered not far from where I lived as a child. Later the head was found and a man was charged with the crime. As it was the school holidays and I had no special plans, I decided to attend the court hearings. It was very gruesome, but after hearing all the evidence I agreed with the jury who found the man guilty of murder.

Another case, which I'm sure attracted attention worldwide and was made into a film, was the case of Azaria Chamberlain who was taken by a dingo at Ayers Rock. Her mother was charged with murder and found guilty. She was sentenced to a lengthy stay in jail, but doubts existed in the minds of many people concerning the jury's decision. Later, Lindy Chamberlain was exonerated and set free. False evidence had been given and it appeared that she had been convicted incorrectly. Then there are cases where it seems that the person charged is guilty, but there is insufficient evidence to prove the case.

Today, in the wealthy Western world, it is difficult to distinguish between the Christian and the non-Christian. Most seem to live in well-built homes, drive expensive cars, wear fine clothes and have plenty of food on the table. The only difference seems to be that certain well-dressed people get up and drive off somewhere at the same time each Sunday morning. The neighbours don't really notice because they are still in bed, or they are also about to set off in their car for a day out. Everyone does their own thing and no one cares, provided what they do does not upset those next door.

If you asked the non-Christian neighbour what was a Christian, he would probably reply, 'Oh, someone who does people good turns.' What evidence

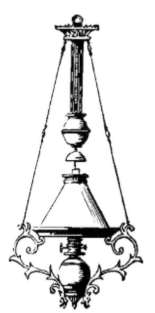

should be seen by the world to prove that you are a Christian? After all, the Lord Jesus said to his followers, 'You are the light of the world. A city that is set on a hill cannot be hidden. Nor do they light a lamp and put it under a basket, but on a lampstand, and it gives light to all who are in the house. Let your light so shine before men, that they may see your good works and glorify your Father in heaven' (Matthew 5:14-16). The apostle Peter urged Christians to live a godly life so that the people round about could 'by [their] good works which they observe, glorify God...' (1 Peter 2:12).

First of all Christians should love God totally (Matthew 22:37), and love their neighbour as themselves. Christ said, 'If anyone loves me, he will keep my word...' (John 14:23). This means by the grace of God we obey the Ten Commandments, and all the other commandments outlined in the Scriptures. Christians are not to be involved in telling unclean stories or using bad language. The next-door neighbour will soon realize that you are different

to his other friends when you take a stand for the law of God. And he will understand why, when you tell him that the reason behind your behaviour is your love of Christ.

Your neighbour will notice that you are there to help him when he is in need. He will also notice that you don't become involved in the 'club' life with all its evils. You don't buy his raffle tickets because you see it as sinful; but he does notice that you are willing to give money freely to worthy organizations in need of financial help.

Christians are people who should not hold grudges against their neighbour, despite the actions of the neighbour against them. They should return good for evil. Yes, your neighbour will notice that you are different to his other friends who live for themselves and their families. Your neighbour will also realize that you are a Christian because he knows you attend worship (carrying your Bible, I trust) each week. He'll know this because you've asked him to attend, or invited his children to attend the Sunday school.

In other words, your neighbour will see you living out what you believe. He will be well aware of why you live as you do, because you have told him. He will also notice that when someone praises you for what you do, you give that praise to Christ. Yes, there is sufficient evidence to prove that you are a Christian. You will simply be doing the works that God pre-determined you should do (Ephesians 2:10).

In today's Western world Christians generally have little influence in society. The church is powerless, because believers are not willing to stand firm for the truth of the Lord Jesus. We don't like upsetting people with the truth, which they dislike. We like to be popular with people and don't want to be disliked because we call the evil of today by its name — sin!

When Christians start to show the fruit of the Spirit in their lives there will be plenty of evidence that they are Christians. That fruit is '…love, joy, peace, longsuffering, kindness, goodness, faithfulness, gentleness, self-control' (Galatians 5:22-23).

141

LORD, who may abide in your tabernacle?
Who may dwell in your holy hill?
He who walks uprightly,
And works righteousness,
And speaks the truth in his heart;
He who does not backbite with his tongue,
Nor does evil to his neighbour,
Nor does he take up a reproach against his friend

(Psalm 15:1-3).

To think about

1. What is a Christian?
2. What evidence is there to prove that your home is a Christian home?
3. In Romans 12:20 we read: 'If your enemy is hungry, feed him; if he is thirsty, give him a drink; for in so doing you will heap coals of fire on his head.' What does this mean?
4. Does your neighbour know that you are a Christian? Why not, or how?

What! The teacher said that!

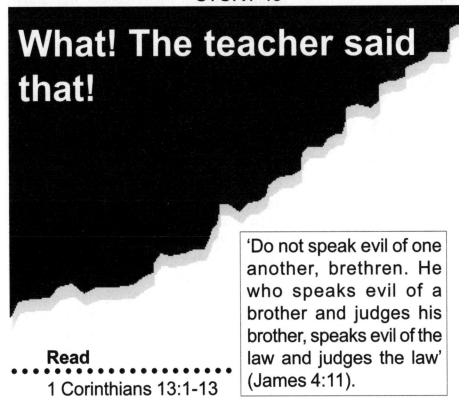

'Do not speak evil of one another, brethren. He who speaks evil of a brother and judges his brother, speaks evil of the law and judges the law' (James 4:11).

Read
• • • • • • • • • • • • • • • • • • • •
1 Corinthians 13:1-13

Many of the world's problems are due to misunderstandings. It is so easy to accuse someone of hurting you when in fact he is totally innocent. We have to be very careful when we speak, as people may not hear well and blame us for saying something we didn't say.

I can remember a parent calling at school to complain about a staff member who was supposed to have called her son a 'scurvy elephant'. She was

very indignant about her child being called such a terrible name. However an investigation soon proved that the teacher had been correcting the child for his behaviour in class and simply said he was a 'disturbing element'.

Only recently I was apologizing to a man who spoke to me some time ago and I had ignored him. Val saw the incident and noticed the strange look on the man's face when I

simply walked by. He could well have thought I had deliberately ignored him.

My wife told me that she had read of a woman who hurriedly left a room with her nose in the air. Several people commented on her proud ways, especially as she had walked out without speaking to anyone. Later they discovered that she had a cold and had quickly left the room as she needed a tissue.

It is so easy to read wrong motives into another person's actions. The Scriptures warn us against such sinful thoughts. Our text plainly says we are not to speak evil of another person, because in doing so we 'speak evil of the law and judge the law'. The law that is spoken of here is God's law of love: 'You shall love your neighbour as yourself' (James 2:8). The person who speaks evil of another is really saying, 'I disagree with God's law of love. I'm going to push God off his throne and I will become the lawmaker.' We change the law from 'Love your neighbour as yourself,' to 'You shall speak evil of other people.'

In today's reading we are told that Christian love 'thinks no evil' (1 Corinthians 13:5). We should think the best of others and be very careful not to misunderstand what another person does or says. If we have a difficulty with a Christian brother or sister, Christ has given us the remedy to overcome it. Open your Bible to Matthew 18:15-17, where you will read that you must go to the brother or sister who you believe has offended you and discuss the matter with him. If you cannot solve the issue you are to take along a Christian friend to assist you in sorting out the matter. He will be a witness to all that is said. If that meeting does not bring the matter to a satisfactory conclusion you hand the dispute over to the church — the elders — and they then will sort out the problem.

We are not to go about criticizing other people. We are to love them all, even our enemies. However, if a Christian brother or sister causes disunity in the church, the time might come when we must have nothing to do with that troublemaker (2 Thessalonians 3:6). The reason behind such an action is to bring the person to their senses so that they might act in a sensible, helpful manner (2 Thessalonians 3:14).

We all need to believe and practise what Paul wrote in today's reading. If everyone acted in this way the world would be a much better place, and the church would win the attention of the world, as people saw the love God's people had for each other.

Let us start by showing Christian love in the family. That often is the hardest place to show the love of God.

In God (I will praise his word),
In God I have put my trust;
I will not fear.
What can flesh do to me?
All day they twist my words;
All their thoughts are against me for evil

(Psalm 56:4-5).

To think about

1. Describe an argument you have had with a person caused by a misunderstanding.
2. We have to be careful how we speak. In Proverbs 11:13 we read: 'A talebearer reveals secrets, but he who is of a faithful spirit conceals a matter.' What does this mean?
3. If you are upset by what someone said or did, what should you do?
4. The Bible tells us that everyone will one day be called to give an account for every word they have spoken. When will this be? Read Matthew 12:36.

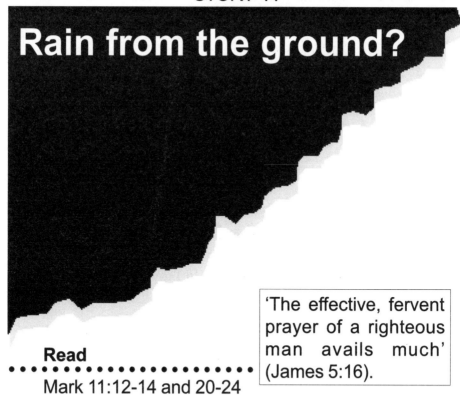

Rain from the ground?

Read
● ● ● ● ● ● ● ● ● ● ● ● ● ● ● ● ● ● ● ●
Mark 11:12-14 and 20-24

'The effective, fervent prayer of a righteous man avails much' (James 5:16).

One of the most difficult commands to obey is the one to 'pray without ceasing' (1 Thessalonians 5:17) to the God who saved us through his Son, the Lord Jesus. Our God is more ready to hear and answer our prayers than we are to ask. When his disciples asked him for a model prayer, Christ replied with what is known as 'The Lord's Prayer' (Matthew 6:9-14). Really, this prayer should be called 'The disciples' prayer'!

Elsewhere guidelines are given for our prayers. The first one is that we ask in Christ's name: 'If you ask anything in my name, I will do it' (John 14:14). He is the Mediator between God and Man, and it is useless to attempt to come to God through the name of Mary or any of the saints or angels. The Scriptures declare: 'For there is one God and one Mediator between God and men, the Man Christ Jesus...' (1 Timothy 2:5).

Then we must pray according to God's will: 'Now this is the confidence that we have in him, that if we ask anything according to his will, he hears us' (1 John 5:14).

We must also be zealous, which is a sign that our prayer truly comes from the heart. Christ told the story of the widow who by her constant approaches to the unjust judge gained a hearing (Luke 18:2-5). God invites us to be the same with him, for he said that we should 'pray and not lose heart' (Luke 18:1).

As we read the Scriptures and discover what God's will is for his people we can pray according to that revealed will and expect an answer. Elijah prayed that the rain would not fall for three and a half years, and this was because God revealed it to him. Daniel prayed that God would return his people to Judah and this was because he knew that the seventy years of captivity was coming to an end — again according to God's revealed will.

However, there are instances of a special prayer of faith. Christ cursed the fig tree and it died. He then invited his disciples also to pray such a prayer. Now it is difficult for us to pray this way and few people have seen God answer what might be called 'an impossible prayer'. The godly George Müller, who was known for his great trust in God, never asked for financial help in his Christian work but always found that God answered his 'impossible' prayers in wonderful ways. On one occasion there was no food on the breakfast table for the orphan children for whom he cared.

The tables were set, but the plates were empty and there was no money with which to buy food. With the children seated and waiting for their meal, Müller lifted his hands heavenward and prayed a prayer of thanksgiving for the food the Lord was about to provide. No sooner had he finished praying than there was a knock on the door, and there stood the local baker with an armful of loaves of bread. He explained that he couldn't sleep that night as he was concerned that the children were without food. As a result, he rose early in the morning and baked some fresh bread for the orphanage.

A few minutes later there was a second knock on the door and the local milkman announced that he had cans of fresh milk for the children. His milk cart had broken down outside the orphanage and, as he had to unload the milk to make repairs, they could have it all. The God of grace had come to Müller's aid when his need was greatest, answering his prayer of faith. George Müller became known as 'the man who gets things from God'.

I would like to mention once again John Paton, the great missionary to the New Hebrides, who prayed what we might call 'the impossible prayer'. He wanted to show the natives that his God was the God of the impossible. The natives had no understanding of obtaining fresh, drinking water from a hole in the ground. To them rain fell from the clouds. You have read just a part of this story in a previous chapter. Here we read more of the prayer of faith of a great man of God.

After much prayer, John announced to the disbelieving natives that he would dig a well, which would produce fresh, drinking water. He had no idea of the spot where he should dig, nor any assurance that there was any subterranean water on the island. But he was fully confident that God would answer his prayer. Much to the concern of the natives John commenced his dig. After some days of prayer and digging he announced that the next day water would be found in the well. The natives feared that the walls of the hole would 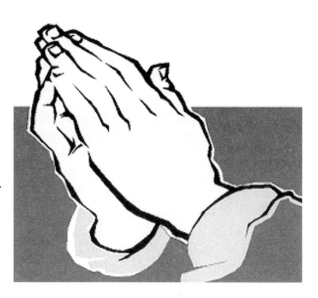 fall in on John and kill him, while others thought he'd dig through the bottom of the island and drop into the sea where he'd be eaten by sharks.

On the day John had said water would appear, he began to dig and the water began to flow into the well. The old chief took a jug of the well water from John, tasted it and declared, 'Rain! Rain! Yes, it's rain! But how did you get it?'

John Paton replied, 'Jehovah my God gave it out of his own earth in answer to our labours and prayers.'

This 'miracle' resulted in a change in the attitude of the natives towards John. God used the water in the well to bring many natives to faith in Christ. This was a prayer of faith. John Paton asked for what seemed an impossibility and God answered.

Our God is the God of the 'impossible' because he has all power in heaven and on earth. He delights to answer the 'impossible' prayers of his people.

That is why Christ said to his disciples: 'For assuredly, I say to you, whoever says to this mountain, "Be removed and be cast into the sea," and does not doubt in his heart, but believes that those things he says will be done, he will have whatever he says' (Mark 11:23).

Many Christians pray without any thought of God's will. They just pray for what they want. We need to thank God for all he has done for us. We must confess our sins and ask for grace to live a righteous life. We need to read God's promises and then 'plead' with him in prayer, asking him to honour his promises that are found in the Scriptures.

Maybe the day will come when God calls upon you to pray that special prayer, asking for the 'impossible'. However, Christian friends, pray on, believing that God will come to your aid. And, non-Christian, you have a special promise in the Scriptures just for you if you are seeking Christ: 'If you then, being evil, know how to give good gifts to your children, how much more will your heavenly Father give the Holy Spirit to those who ask him' (Luke 11:13). May God bless you!

I love the LORD, because he has heard
My voice and my supplications.
Because he has inclined his ear to me,
Therefore I will call upon him as long as I live

(Psalm 116:1-2).

To think about

1. What is prayer?
2. What are some of God's rules for prayer that his people must follow?
3. Discuss any 'impossible' prayer that God answered.
4. To help you remember things and people you should pray for, make a list.

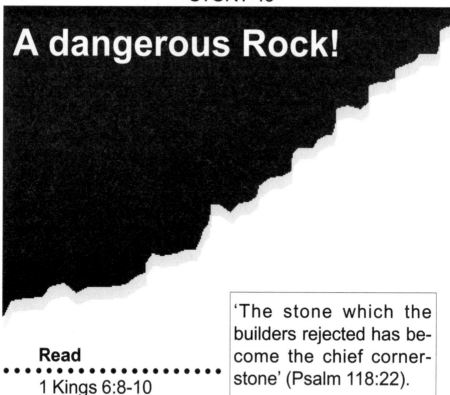

A dangerous Rock!

Read
• • • • • • • • • • • • • • • • • • • •
1 Kings 6:8-10

'The stone which the builders rejected has become the chief cornerstone' (Psalm 118:22).

Often in the Scriptures we find the Lord Jesus compared to a rock. The Pharisees and their supporters were warned against opposing the Rock that they had rejected. Christ warned them very plainly: 'The stone which the

builders rejected has become the chief cornerstone. This was the LORD's doing, and it is marvellous in our eyes. Therefore I say to you, the kingdom of God will be taken from you and given to a nation bearing the fruits of it. And whoever falls on this stone will be broken; but on whomever it falls, it will grind him to powder' (Matthew 21:42-44).

The kingdoms of the world have been mighty, but they do not last. In the days of King Nebuchadnezzar, Daniel interpreted the king's dream where he prophesied the world's mighty empires would come and go. However, there was one kingdom

'which shall never be destroyed' (Daniel 2:44). A stone that fell from the huge statue destroyed the last great world empire, and in turn established another worldwide kingdom. The stone that fell was none other than the Lord Jesus. His kingdom is the church, against which Satan and his demons cannot have the victory: 'the stone that struck the image became a great mountain and filled the whole earth' (Daniel 2:35). Christ's kingdom is a kingdom made from people from every part of the world. In Revelation 7:9 we read a description of that realm: 'After these things I looked, and behold, a great multitude which no one could number, of all nations, tribes, peoples, and tongues, standing before the throne and before the Lamb...' It was the Jewish people who rejected Christ, who was the chief cornerstone of the realm that he was building.

There is a story about the rejection of the chief cornerstone, which happened when the great temple of Solomon was being constructed. From your reading you will know that the building blocks were cut well away from the construction site. With the first load of blocks the builders found one which didn't seem to fit into the plans for that stage of the work. They put the stone to one side and continued working. When the walls had almost been completed, the workmen sent for the cornerstone that they expected to be amongst one of the last loads of building blocks. The masons sent word that the precious cornerstone was amongst the first load of stones sent to the construction site. The workmen then found that the stone they had put to one side, many months before, was the one they needed.

Soon the cornerstone was in its place, holding the walls in the correct position and ensuring that the temple would not fall down. The Pharisees would have nothing to do with Messiah and his kingdom and planned to have him killed. But they were warned by Christ of the danger of their plan: 'And whoever falls on this stone will be broken; but on whomever it falls, it will grind him to powder' (Matthew 21:44). Here we have the picture of the all-powerful Christ as he deals with his enemies.

Those who oppose the Lord Jesus and his kingdom may fall upon him with all the violence they can muster, but he is not hurt. The one who falls upon the Rock is the one who is hurt. Others who have tried to destroy the church have come under judgement — the Rock falls upon them. The result is that they are ground to powder!

The Pharisees, who heard our Lord speak those words, had just heard him tell the parable of the wicked vinedressers who had killed the landowner's son. They knew he spoke this parable about them and they wanted him out of the way. They would kill him. But where are those unrepentant Pharisees today? They are not in heaven!

Of this glorious Rock, Peter wrote: 'Behold, I lay in Zion a chief cornerstone, elect, precious, and he who believes on him will by no means be put to shame' (1 Peter 2:6). The Lord Jesus is the Rock of our salvation and our faith in him will never result in shame to us.

> The stone which the builders rejected
> Has become the chief cornerstone.
> This was the LORD's doing;
> It is marvellous in our eyes.
> This is the day the LORD has made;
> We will rejoice and be glad in it
>
> (Psalm 118:22-24).

To think about

1. Who was King Nebuchadnezzar?
2. Read Matthew 16:13-19 and state who or what you think is the rock upon which Christ would build his church.
3. Name one Pharisee who came to faith in the Lord Jesus (Acts chapter 9 and John 19:39).
4. In Psalm 95 we read of one who is 'the Rock of our salvation'. Who is this 'Rock'?

A cranky bull

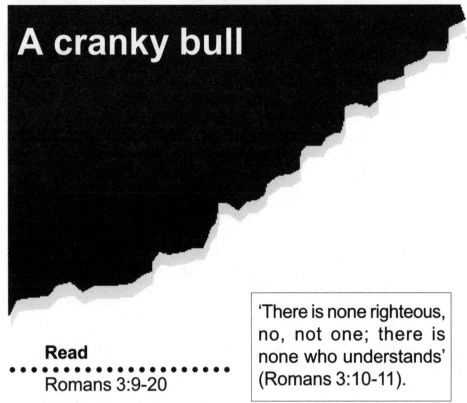

Read
• • • • • • • • • • • • • • • • • •
Romans 3:9-20

'There is none righteous, no, not one; there is none who understands' (Romans 3:10-11).

Most people look at themselves in the mirror each day and think that they are not such bad people after all. They have a wash, dress, clean their teeth, comb their hair and again have a look in the mirror to make sure they look their best and off they go to the day's activities. Others go to extremes to cover the wrinkles, dye the grey hair and make themselves look better than they do in front of the mirror when they wake, because they don't like what they see.

A farmer friend had a small herd of cattle, which he raised for the butcher. They were fed a special diet and often were allowed into the field near the house. The cows would eat the lush grass, but one day the bull had a different idea. He wandered up close to the house and suddenly saw a reflection in the glass patio doors. He threw his head from side

153

to side and snorted, blowing froth from his mouth and nostrils. He didn't like what he saw. I guess he saw another bull who was snorting and throwing his head about in an angry mood. My friend and his wife heard the noise and came to the side of the house to watch the display of anger. They quietly

laughed at the silly bull who was becoming more agitated by what he saw. He scratched dirt over his shoulder just as my friends realized that something disastrous was about to happen.

Before they could shout and chase the bull away, he charged at the glass door. There was a crash as the bull hit his reflection and the steel upright that held it all in place. A shower of glass went up in the air and the bull staggered back, shaking his head and looking for his opponent who had really hurt him. Seeing no other bull and two humans running at him, waving their hands and shouting, he decided to retreat. Then came the expense of a workman replacing the glass. The bull was never popular after that event and was barred from that field from that day on.

Have you ever seen a reflection of what you are spiritually like — what you are like in God's eyes? Today's reading is like a mirror because it tells the ungodly what they are truly like in God's eyes. I'm sure that many unsaved people read these words and totally disagree with what they see. Of course there are some people who see the passage as a reflection of their character. As they continue reading they realize they need a change in character, especially as they must one day face the God who sees them as the Scriptures describe.

We can't do anything to change how God sees us, but God can! Sinners need to be changed by the Holy Spirit. Ezekiel wrote the words of God: 'I will cleanse you from all your filthiness and from all your idols. I will give you a new heart and put a new spirit within you; I will take the heart of stone out of your flesh and give you a heart of flesh. I will put my Spirit within you and cause you to walk in my statutes, and you will keep my judgements and do them' (Ezekiel 36:25-27).

The change of heart is the work of God alone and sinners are unable to do anything to earn the grace of God. Some people think that if only they can believe in Christ, God will be obliged to put his Spirit in their heart; but this is not so. It is the Holy Spirit who freely gives faith to those who are called of God. Nicodemus was told this great truth (John 3:5-8). God changes our character in his sight by crediting the perfect righteousness of the Lord Jesus Christ to our account. We are justified!

It is the Holy Spirit who then sanctifies believers in their daily walk with their Lord. The saints are the holy ones, who by the grace of God turn from their sins, and delight in obedience. When we look into God's mirror, we see our sinful ways, but God looks at us through his Son and we are seen to be holy. What a wonderful God we have!

> The fool has said in his heart,
> 'There is no God.'
> They are corrupt,
> They have done abominable works,
> There is none who does good.
> The LORD looks down from heaven upon the children of men,
> To see if there are any who understand, who seek God.
> They have all turned aside,
> They have together become corrupt;
> There is none who does good,
> No, not one
>
> (Psalm 14:1-3).

To think about

1. What is sin?
2. What is meant by the word 'regeneration'?
3. What makes it possible for a sinner to break away from his sinful ways?
4. Discuss some of the proofs we have that there is a God.

Get out of your home before it's too late!

Read
• • • • • • • • • • • • • • • • • • •
Luke 23:32-43

'Behold, now is the accepted time; behold, now is the day of salvation' (2 Corinthians 6:2).

There are many people who are always running late in their activities. Others never seem to complete their work. Of course there are some who are never late in anything they do. To which group do you belong?

In 1955 the Hunter Valley of New South Wales, Australia, suffered very severe flooding. At that time we lived in our family home on the farm and had water six feet deep inside the house. We all had to move out until the water had receded and then we could return to clean up the mess.

I would like to tell you about the people who lived in Mount Pleasant Street, Maitland. This was indeed a very pleasant street with very comfortable homes built on either side. The rains fell and

the warnings were given that big floods were on their way. There was a sharp bend in the river and it was feared that the flooded Hunter River would burst its banks and flood Mount Pleasant Street with raging, muddy water.

The police visited each home, urging the occupants to move out before they were trapped; but many people simply refused to leave and before long they realized they had left it too late. They were like the 'rich fool' who thought he could enjoy his retirement without any fear of death. But the call came from God that he was required for judgement and he died (Luke 12:16-21). He had left repentance too late.

The two thieves who were crucified beside the Lord Jesus had neglected to make peace with God. They were like the foolish people in Mount Pleasant Street who woke up during the night to find that water was already inside their homes. Those people suddenly realized they were trapped and when the protective levee banks collapsed under the pressure of the raging flood the water inside their homes rose, destroying their possessions. People were forced to climb up through the manhole and into the ceiling and then onto the roof where they waited for daylight. The water swirled around their homes and onwards towards the long cement bridge that connected the city to the hospital and beyond.

As the sun rose it became obvious that their lives were in danger. The men with rowing boats found it impossible to row to the people, so hundreds gathered to watch the unfolding drama. The swiftly flowing floodwater suddenly lifted a wooden house off its foundations and swept it to the bridge where it was smashed to pieces. This was followed by other houses with people clinging to whatever they could. A few people were rescued at the bridge, while others were swept into the flooded farmland areas where some drowned.

The people had ignored the warnings to leave their homes, but now warnings meant nothing. I'm sure that many said to themselves as they were swept away, 'If only…'

The two thieves on the cross knew they were facing death and God's judgement. They had ignored the warnings to repent of their sins and it looked as if they had left their eternal well-being too late.

There, nailed to a cross beside a person called Jesus, they were about to die. As they looked to Jesus they saw a person, naked, bleeding from nail wounds and a severe whipping. He didn't look like a king, but one thief recognized him as being both a king and having a kingdom.

As death stared him in the face he turned to King Jesus and said, 'Lord, remember me when you come into your kingdom' (Luke 23:42). His cry for salvation came late, but not too late! He heard the comforting words of Christ, 'Assuredly, I say to you, today you will be with me in paradise' (Luke 23:43). He was like those people from Mount Pleasant Street who were rescued at the very last moment. The other criminal beside the Saviour died unrepentant.

We all need to remember the scriptural truth, '…it is appointed for men to die once, but after this the judgement' (Hebrews 9:27). None should leave the making of peace with God until it is too late. We should all treat very seriously the words of the apostle Paul, 'Behold, now is the day of salvation' (2 Corinthians 6:2). For any one of us there may be no tomorrow!

Oh come, let us worship and bow down;
Let us kneel before the LORD our Maker.
For he is our God,
And we are the people of his pasture,
And the sheep of his hand.
Today, if you will hear his voice:
'Do not harden your hearts, as in the rebellion'

(Psalm 95:6-8).

To think about

1. When is the time we should repent of our sins?
2. What is God's way of saving sinners?
3. One criminal was saved and the other lost. What does this teach us about the God of grace?
4. What does it mean to be saved?

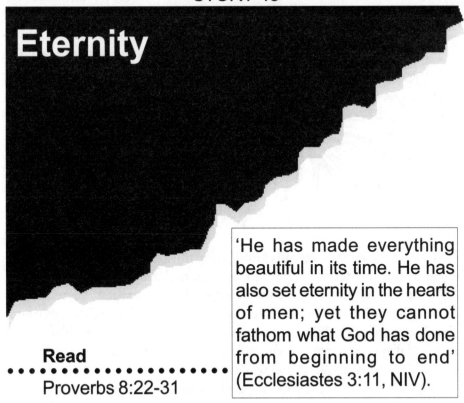

Eternity

'He has made everything beautiful in its time. He has also set eternity in the hearts of men; yet they cannot fathom what God has done from beginning to end' (Ecclesiastes 3:11, NIV).

Read
• • • • • • • • • • • • • • • • • • •
Proverbs 8:22-31

Some time ago there were worldwide celebrations as the year 1999 came to an end and we commenced the year 2000. I'm sure many people sat through hours of TV to watch the various activities in distant parts of the world. The

fireworks were very colourful and there were many 'Oohs' and 'Aahs' as people looked heavenward watching the best display they had ever seen. I feel sure that what was seen in Sydney, Australia, was the best in the world. People could see the Sydney Harbour Bridge in all its glory, as rockets took their loads of explosive into the sky. In the harbour thousands of boats were anchored in the best possible spots to view the 'show of the century or millennium'.

In all the celebrations, which were supposed to commemorate the end of the old millennium and the start of the third millennium, the name of our Saviour, the Lord Jesus, was noticeably absent. This was so disappointing, especially as the majority of the world's citizens have dated time from the birth of the Son of God.

However, in Sydney, the world saw a word in lights splashed across the Sydney Harbour Bridge, and I feel certain that the vast majority of people watching had no idea of its significance. That word was 'Eternity'. We live in time, but the day is coming when Christ returns and time is no more, because we move into God's time zone — eternity! Following the great Judgement Day every human will enter eternity in heaven, or in eternal death — hell.

As we look about us we see the beauty of God's creation. There is order in the organization of this universe, and daily we see the mighty acts of our God. The grace of God shines through even the darkest hours of history and the world displays ample evidence of the God who created all things. All we need to do is look about us and take in the wonder of creation.

Despite what we see about us we know that we are just part of history that is passing and the day will come when we have no part to play in the activities of the world. We are just another part of God's creation, but God has put 'eternity in the hearts of men'. All people have a feeling that there is life beyond the grave. And God has given us the Scriptures, which clearly tell us what to expect and what we must do if we would have a place in his kingdom.

Eternity

'Eternity' was the trademark of a small man, Arthur Stace. He was born in 1884 and both of his parents were drunkards. He had two sisters and two brothers, all of whom loved strong drink. His brothers spent time in jail and his sisters ran brothels. In his childhood Arthur often slept under the house on a bed of bags and was forced to steal food in order to survive.

His early life was spent drinking beer and wine, and at times he found himself locked up in jail. In his twenties he often carried alcohol from the local pubs to places of vice in the area. He helped at the gambling houses and was involved in organized theft. He often wanted to give up the drink, but knew he lacked the power.

During the First World War he served in the army in France, but then returned to Australia and his old way of life. During the depression, cold and hungry, he heard that a cup of tea and some rock cakes were freely available for the 'down and outs' at St Barnabas' Church, at Broadway, Sydney. Archdeacon Hammond conducted a service.

At the service Arthur noticed the difference between the 'down and outs' and the pleasant, kind Christians who served the meals. It was there that he prayed that he could become a Christian. Later he said that he had come to have some rock cakes, but had met the 'Rock of Ages'. He gave up the strong drink, obtained work and began to regain his self-respect. This was in 1930.

In 1932, at a Baptist church in Darlinghurst, Sydney, he heard the 'hellfire' evangelist, Reverend John Ridley, preach. During his sermon he repeatedly used the word 'Eternity' saying, 'I wish I could shout "Eternity" through the streets of Sydney!'

Eternity

At that moment Arthur felt called to let the citizens of Sydney know the word 'Eternity'. He was not at that time a capable speaker, but knew that he was called to write the word where people would be called to meditate on its implications.

Thus Arthur Stace began a lifelong work of writing the word 'Eternity' in chalk in beautiful copperplate writing on the streets of Sydney. He was also involved in street evangelism and doing those works of faith that brought honour to the Lord Jesus. It was not until 1956 that he was caught in the act of writing his word by a Baptist minister. The minister, late at night (for that was when Arthur carried out his evangelism), saw him write his word and asked, 'Are you Mr Eternity?'

Arthur's reply was simply, 'Guilty, your honour.'

Arthur Stace died on 30 July 1967. He is still remembered as the much loved 'Mr Eternity'. On 1 January 2000, Sydney remembered that godly man in its celebrations, but I wonder how many people realized the significance of that one word, Eternity?

Our God is an eternal God. He had no beginning and has no end. He is the great 'I AM'. Eternal life can be obtained through the Lord Jesus who died upon the cross in the place of all his people. It is the Holy Spirit who changes our heart and gives us saving faith in Christ.

When you begin to think of eternity and what will happen to you when you die, do you feel uneasy? The great Augustine said of his God, 'Our hearts are restless till they find their rest in Thee.'

Perfect peace of soul is found in the Lord Jesus. May each of you know the God of peace.

> I will love you, O LORD, my strength.
> The LORD is my rock and my fortress and my deliverer;
> My God, my strength, in whom I will trust;
> My shield and the horn of my salvation, my stronghold.
> I will call upon the LORD, who is worthy to be praised;
> So shall I be saved from my enemies

(Psalm 18:1-3).

To think about

1. What does the word 'eternity' mean?
2. When will you move into eternity?
3. What two eternal dwelling places are there for all humans?
4. Where will the godly spend eternity?
5. What did God mean when he told Moses his name was 'I AM'?

Beware of big fish!

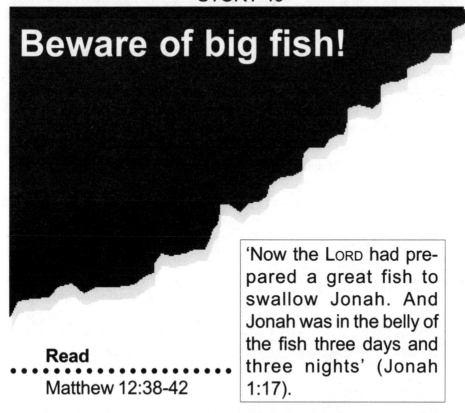

Read
••••••••••••••••••••
Matthew 12:38-42

'Now the LORD had prepared a great fish to swallow Jonah. And Jonah was in the belly of the fish three days and three nights' (Jonah 1:17).

Recently our Bible study group has been looking at the book of Jonah. There were two memories that came flooding back as we commenced our study, and I was pleased to be able to tell our group of the incidents. The first was when I was a 'non teaching' school principal. I had no class to teach, but on occasions visited classrooms to talk to the children.

In one class I asked what I thought would be an easy question: 'Who was the Bible character who was swallowed by a large fish?' I thought most children would know the answer, but to my surprise not one child attempted to respond, because no one knew the answer. I then truly realized I was living in an age where the Bible was largely a forgotten book.

He tasted very nice!

When I was young most people attended church on Sunday. I can remember how the farmers refrained from farm work on the Lord's Day, other than milking the cows. I'm sure that many were not Christians, but everyone went to worship. And almost every child went to Sunday school.

When my children were young, most children went to Sunday school if not to church. Parents believed that their children needed some morality and that came from the teaching they received at Sunday school. But now only a few people attend worship or Sunday school. The church and the teaching of the Bible is largely ignored. When no one in the class knew that Jonah was swallowed by a large fish, I realized what was happening in this careless world. No wonder we are in such a mess today. However, I'm encouraged because I know that God rules the world through the Lord Jesus Christ, who has all power in heaven and on earth.

WHALER

The second memory was of a report I had once read of a sailor who had been swallowed by a whale and later rescued alive. We were discussing Jonah and his rather horrifying tale when I told my group of the story I had read and said I would find it and read it to them. Then came the difficulty of looking, as I couldn't remember where I had read it. After some time I found the book and read the tale to my Christian friends.

The story was of a sailor who in 1931 was on a whaling expedition. The whale being chased smashed their boat and as the sailor was flung into the water he found himself going down the throat of the whale, still alive, but terrified at his plight. Soon he became unconscious. Two days later the whale was harpooned, and as it was being cut open, there lay the man, who was still breathing. His body had been burnt by the acid in the whale's stomach, but after some medical treatment he recovered. I can well imagine that he never ever went whaling again!

We are not told that Jonah was swallowed by a whale, but rather that God prepared a large fish to swallow him. It could well have been a whale, particularly as there is a species of whale which, when facing death, vomits the contents of its stomach up on the beach before it expires. I don't know if that is what happened in Jonah's case, but the very fact that such could happen means that the story of Jonah is very believable.

However, it was God who prepared the large fish to swallow Jonah for the three days and three nights, during which time he repented of his disobedience and promised God he would serve him faithfully in the future. I'm sure every time Jonah saw a fish he would have been reminded of the events of that planned journey from Joppa to Tarshish.

When Jonah preached in Nineveh many people turned to God and were saved. No doubt we will meet those people in heaven where we will hear the story of Jonah from them.

The story of the prophet Jonah was important to the Jews, as he was the sign given to the scribes and Pharisees when they asked Jesus for a sign to prove he was from God and was the long-awaited Messiah. Jesus said to them, 'For as Jonah was three days and three nights in the belly of the great fish, so will the Son of Man be three days and three nights in the heart of the earth' (Matthew 12:40).

We read of many miracles in the Scriptures, but Jonah is one of the best known. Let us each play our part in introducing young people to those great Bible characters. At the same time let us remember that they also need to meet the one who lay in the tomb for three days and rose again, the Lord Jesus Christ. May we all be witnesses to the saving grace of the Lord Jesus.

Save me, O God!
For the waters have come up to my neck.
I sink in deep mire,
Where there is no standing;
I have come into deep waters,
Where the floods overflow me.
I am weary with my crying;
My throat is dry;
My eyes fail while I wait for my God

(Psalm 69:1-3).

To think about

1. What special work was Jonah given by God to carry out?
2. Where was it that he repented of his sin of disobedience?
3. Of what great nation was Nineveh the capital city?
4. Of what was Jonah's time in the belly of the large fish, a sign?
5. Why do young people go to Sunday school?
6. Why do people go to the Sunday church service?

[1] *Science returns to God*, James H. Jauncey, Zondervan Publishing House, USA, 1961, pp. 81-82.

Their wives will solve your problem, Jim!

'For there is one God and one Mediator between God and men, the Man Christ Jesus, who gave himself a ransom for all' (1 Timothy 2:5-6).

Read
• •
Numbers 14:11-25

There are many times in our daily life when we use a mediator. Sometimes, when I wish to speak to the doctor and haven't made an appointment I ask the secretary if she would ask him something on my behalf. Away she goes and later returns with the answer I need. I'm sure there are times when you have asked someone to help you out of a distressing problem, by speaking to your mum or dad on your behalf.

The reading today is about Moses, the great leader of the Israelites, who was the one through whom God spoke to his people. God gave Moses the commandments and he then read them to the covenant people. There were times when he prayed to God on behalf of the sinful and complaining Israelites.

Today's reading is about Moses pleading with God on behalf of the Israelites who refused to go into the promised land. They were afraid of what they would find there and disbelieved God when he said he had given them the land for their possession. They even said they would rather have remained in Egypt.

In his anger God told Moses he would destroy the people and then make a new nation of his descendants. Moses prayed on behalf of Israel that God would forgive them once again. In today's passage of Scripture we read the words of Moses pleading for the covenant people. Moses was a true mediator for the children of Israel.

166

I once used some ladies as mediators to get new carpet in the church manse. I had taken up residence in the manse while Val was still in our home, getting things ready for the move. The manse had been painted, but the floor was covered by worn-out carpet. I approached the deacons one day and suggested that it would be better if there was a new carpet on the floor before my family moved in. In our own home we had the floors covered with carpet and I thought the manse floor covering had seen better days.

The men visited the manse and looked at the newly painted walls and thought all looked well. I pointed at the worn-out carpet, but the men said, 'Oh, there's nothing wrong with that. It will last many more years.'

I didn't know what to do, but still believed it needed replacing. I told my brother John about my dilemma and asked for his wise suggestion. His reply was simple.

'Don't bother with the deacons, Jim. Men don't notice these things. Ask their wives into the manse after the night service and they will understand. They will solve your problem!'

The next Sunday, I invited some of the ladies to look over the manse. They commented on the good job that was done with the painting, but when I pointed to the carpet they understood my plight.

'Val can't be expected to live with that!' was the comment.

The next day the 'women mediators' had done their work. Their husbands had been convinced and soon a carpet layer was there. When Val arrived the manse looked much more comfortable. The ladies were ideal mediators in that they knew my wife and also had the attention of their deacon husbands. They did what I could not do.

There is only one mediator between God and men, the man Christ Jesus. He is the perfect Mediator because he is both God and man in the one person. As perfect man he understands our needs, and as God he is able to present our needs to our heavenly Father.

The writer to the Hebrews wrote of Christ our Mediator, 'For we do not have a High Priest who cannot sympathize with our weaknesses, but was in all points tempted as we are, yet without sin. Let us therefore come boldly to the throne of grace, that we may obtain mercy and find grace to help in the time of need' (Hebrews 4:15-16). In the days of the Old Testament the High Priest acted as a mediator between the people and God. He offered sacrifice once each year for the sins of the people, after he had offered sacrifice for his own sin. Now Christ is our great High Priest!

Christ has both the ear of men and women, boys and girls, and the ear of his Father in heaven. When we ask anything of God we must come in the name of the one and only Mediator, the Lord Jesus. He presents our requests to his Father and, through Jesus, God blesses his people.

Take no notice of anyone who would suggest that there are other mediators: angels, saints, popes or even Mary, the beloved mother of Jesus. Our text is very plain and easy to understand: the Holy Spirit has declared that 'there is one God and one Mediator between God and men, the Man Christ Jesus, who gave himself a ransom for all' (1 Timothy 2:5-6).

We have a wonderful Mediator!

The LORD has sworn
And will not relent,
'You are a priest forever
According to the order of Melchizedek'

(Psalm 110:4).

To think about

1. Who is the only Mediator between God and men?
2. Why is he able to be such a perfect Mediator?
3. What does Jesus do with your prayers?
4. In what way was Moses a mediator for the children of Israel?
5. Can you think of any situation where you acted as a mediator for others?

A well-travelled fish

Read
• • • • • • • • • • • • • • • • • • • •
Matthew 25:31-46

'Then I heard a voice from heaven saying to me, "Write: 'Blessed are the dead who die in the Lord from now on'." "Yes," says the Spirit, "that they may rest from their labours, and their works follow them"' (Revelation 14:13).

Wherever I walk around the house or the garden, I have a little shadow that faithfully follows me — my dog Wags. At my study table he lies down at my feet and if I rest in bed he hops up beside me and lies at the foot of the bed.

Some people are followed everywhere by their children or grandchildren. We are also all followed by our character, so we need to be on guard all the time.

Our text reminds us that the knowledge of our works follow us into eternity and are all recorded in one of God's books. If we really believed this we would be more conscious of the need to live a holy life at all times. The saints are workers in God's building whose foundation is Jesus Christ and

the apostles and prophets. Some faithful Christians do a great work, while others who are lazy produce little of lasting value.

Someone has written that there are four groups in the church, each which can be likened to a bone.

The wishbones: those who spend the day wishing that others would do the work;
The jawbones: those who do all the talking;
The knucklebones: those who knock everything; and
The backbones: those who do the work.

We are told that Judgement Day will reveal the value of the work we have carried out. While these words have special application to ministers they speak to all Christians: 'Now if anyone builds on this foundation with gold, silver, precious stones, wood, hay, straw, each one's work will become clear; for the day will declare it, because it will be revealed by fire; and the fire will test each one's work, of what sort it is. If anyone's work which he has built on it endures, he will receive a reward. If anyone's work is burned, he will suffer loss; but he himself will be saved, yet so as through fire' (1 Corinthians 3:12-15).

One of my close fishing mates was transferred to another state and as a joke he hid a dead fish under our house. After a couple of days the fish made

its presence known. However, the practical joker had left a rather large, old cupboard for us to have transported by train to his new home and I thought the fish should be returned to its owner. I opened the cupboard door and nailed the smelly, rotting fish to one of the shelves and locked the door. A week later my mate collected the cupboard to discover that his fish had followed him. It certainly was a well-travelled fish!

When I visited his home several years later he took me to the cupboard that was under his house and opening the door said, 'Have a sniff!'

Sure enough, not only had the rotting fish followed him, but its smell was still in the wood. He explained how he and his wife had washed the cupboard many times with sweet smelling liquid, but the smell of the stinking fish could not be removed. I think the odour will be with that cupboard till the day it is burned!

On Judgement Day we are told that we will be judged, 'each one according to his works' (Revelation 20:13). The works that matter will be those done in the name of the Lord Jesus Christ and out of love for both God and man. I once read:

Only one life, and it will soon be passed;
Only what's done for Christ will last.

Our Bible reading explains very clearly that those works done in the name of Christ and for our Christian brothers and sisters will be as if they were done for Christ himself. He then will reward his people accordingly. Christ will welcome his faithful people with the gracious words: 'Come, you blessed of my Father, inherit the kingdom prepared for you from the foundation of the world' (Matthew 25:34).

Those who failed to minister to others in the name of Christ will 'go away into everlasting punishment...' (Matthew 25:46). The saints will be rewarded for doing the works that God ordained that they should do (Ephesians 2:10). Those works are the outcome of saving faith and without them our life would show that our 'faith' is a dead faith. James wrote: 'For as the body without the spirit is dead, so faith without works is dead also' (2:26).

All who have confessed their faith in Christ Jesus should take note of Paul's words to the Christians at Philippi: '...work out your own salvation with fear and trembling; for it is God who works in you both to will and to do for his good pleasure' (Philippians 2:12-13).

May we all serve our Lord and Saviour, Jesus Christ, with diligence, simply because we love him. The motivation for the good works must never be to obtain a reward — No! Our good works are the result of our love of Christ and the joy we have in carrying out his commandments.

Let the heavens rejoice, and let the earth be glad;
Let the sea roar, and all its fullness;
Let the field be joyful, and all that is in it.
Then all the trees of the woods will rejoice before the LORD.
For he is coming, for he is coming to judge the earth.
He shall judge the world with righteousness,
And the peoples with his truth

(Psalm 96:11-13).

To think about

1. Why has God made a record of everything we do and say?
2. Can you think of some of your works that were made of 'diamonds' and others of 'hay'?
3. What makes a work to be recognized as having been made of 'gold' and another of 'hay'?
4. When will Christ judge the world in righteousness?

A bumpy landing

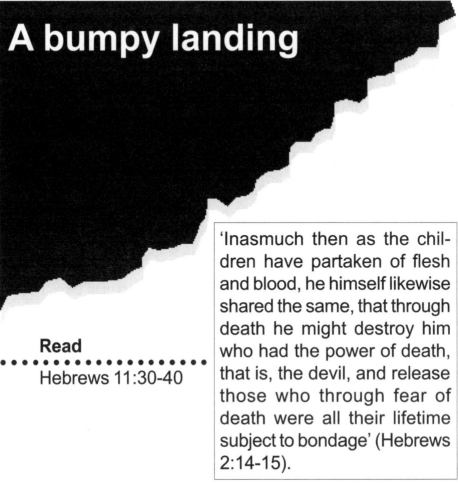

Read

• • • • • • • • • • • • • • • • • • • •

Hebrews 11:30-40

'Inasmuch then as the children have partaken of flesh and blood, he himself likewise shared the same, that through death he might destroy him who had the power of death, that is, the devil, and release those who through fear of death were all their lifetime subject to bondage' (Hebrews 2:14-15).

I find travel by aeroplane very uncomfortable because I have an unreasonable fear of heights while the rest of the family seem unconcerned. Travel by air is a last resort for me, but when we decided to take our first trip overseas, it was the only way to go. Our flights were booked and eventually Val and I, plus our two youngest daughters, were in the airport lounge. We were there an hour or so before departure to check in and select our seats. I chose a seat in the middle of the plane so I couldn't see out of a window while the others were as close to the window as possible.

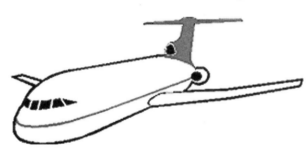

While we waited Val kept pointing to the huge planes and as the talk became more excited I noticed I was starting to perspire. My hands were very moist so I kept reading my book.

But I noticed that people were moving about everywhere in the airport terminal. I began to think that the terminal was just like the world. There were people of all ages going about their business. Some were eating meals, many were talking and laughing while others seemed concerned about booking tickets and having their luggage put in the correct place for their flight. Everyone seemed to have something to do and most were having a great time while I sat there and worried about the fact that when I was thirty thousand metres up in the sky there was about two centimetres of steel and aluminium supporting me.

I watched as people arrived and departed from the airport. I thought, 'That's like the world. People are born and others die. We all come and go.' I was thinking that not everyone had tickets, which I likened to our God-given faith, which is our passport to heaven.

Some people worked at the airport, others had come to see friends off and one person was telling the clerk he had forgotten the tickets for his family. His wife and children didn't seem very happy about the situation. That reminded me of a joke about some people who were checking in. They had all their bags ready to board their plane. As the husband was going through the list he said, 'I wish I had brought the refrigerator with us.'

His wife looked at him and replied, 'Don't be silly! Why would we need that?'

His reply was simple: 'Because I left our tickets on top of the refrigerator.'

Then I watched the planes landing and taking off. 'That's like death,' I thought to myself. Some landings were very smooth, reminding me that many Christians have a quiet death, as did Hudson Taylor, who just took a deep breath as he was in his bed and passed into glory.

As I was watching, a plane made a very heavy landing. Smoke blew out from the tyres as they hit the tarmac very heavily. The plane bounced and Val and the girls laughed and said, 'Boy! Did you see that, Dad! I hope he's not our pilot!'

I watched very closely and, sure enough, the plane came to our boarding space. But that rough landing reminded me of Christians who faced a painful death, as did Stephen who was stoned (Acts 7:54-60). Our reading passage records the terrible death endured by some of the martyrs.

As our flight was ready, I took the tablet the doctor had given me to calm my nerves, and walked towards the plane. I sat in my seat, head down, reading my book, but I couldn't help thinking, 'This plane is sure to crash!'

Death is a curse. It is the wages of sin and the last enemy to be destroyed. However, no matter how death comes we should remember that Christ has removed its sting, which is sin (1 Corinthians 15:56-57). Christians should not fear death itself, even though the process of dying may be unpleasant. Death means being with Christ as the apostle Paul said, 'For to me, to live is Christ, and to die is gain ... [to] be with Christ, which is far better' (Philippians 1:21, 23).

The ungodly Voltaire's last words, as death was about to take him, were, 'I am abandoned by God and man. I shall go to hell!' Then looking at the flames of the candle burning on the table beside his bed he added, 'The flames already?'

For Christians facing death, the fear has been removed, as we can tell from the dying words of some of the saints:

'I am going to see the King in all his glory!'

'The chariot has come, and I am ready to step in.'

'Can this be death? Why, it is better than living. Tell them I die happy in Jesus.'

It is worth reading the description of the death of Christian and Hopeful in *Pilgrim's Progress*. Satan made Christian's death difficult, but Hopeful passed over in peace. There in the Promised Land they entered the city of God, 'and lo, as they entered, they were transfigured: and they had raiment put on that shone like Gold...Then I heard in my dream, that all the bells in the City rang again for joy; and that it was said unto them, "Enter ye into the joy of our Lord." I also heard the men themselves say, that they sang with a loud voice, saying, "Blessing, Honour, Glory, and Power, be to Him that sitteth upon the throne, and to the Lamb, for ever and ever." '

Friends, our Lord has promised never to leave us nor forsake us — no, neither in life nor death. We must just trust his words and rest in him to do what is right.

May we all be able to face death with a true confidence in our heart, because our Redeemer has removed its sting. May God bless you all.

Precious in the sight of the LORD
Is the death of his saints

(Psalm 116:15).

To think about

1. Why can the Christian face death with confidence in his heart?
2. What is death?
3. What happens to the Christian when he dies?
4. Why do you think some people fear death?
5. What can you do to ensure you face death with a joy in your heart?

If you have read this book, why not send a postcard of your homeland to me at the following address?

James A. Cromarty
3 Appaloosa Place
Wingham
N. S. W. 2429
Australia